PACIFIC COAST HIGHWAY

Also by Tom Snyder

Route 66 Traveler's Guide and Roadside Companion

PACIFIC
COAST
HIGHWAY
TRAVELER'S GUIDE

TOM SNYDER

ST. MARTIN'S GRIFFIN 🙠 NEW YORK

www.stmartins.com

In using this guide, please be assured that no fees are accepted by either author or publisher for any listings or recommendations appearing herein.

Copyedit by Rebecca Pieken

Jacket design by the author

FRONT COVER: Woodie/US 101 logo based in part on a photograph by Forrest L. Doud, with art direction by Dan Sweet. Courtesy of Pismo Beach Convention and Visitors Bureau.

BACK COVER: Washington Rainforest, courtesy of North Olympic Peninsula Visitors and Convention Bureau. Oregon Cloudfall, courtesy of the author. California Coast, courtesy of Suzie Lankes—Magdalena Palmer, Photographer. The Del, courtesy of Hotel Del Coronado.

PHOTO CREDITS:
Page 58: Santa Cruz County Conference and Visitors Council. Page 100: Eureka! Convention and Visitors Bureau—Jack Hopkins, Photographer. Page 103: San Francisco Convention and Visitors Bureau. Page 125: Oregon Tourism—Steve Terrill, Photographer. Page 134: Bay Area Chamber of Commerce—Jason Stoll, Photographer. Page 148: Long Beach Peninsula Visitors Bureau. Page 153: Port Townsend Chamber of Commerce. Page 170: O'Sofsky & Shea—John Shea, Photographer (1935). Page 173: Paso Robles Inn (1946). Page 183: Barnstorming Adventures. Remaining photographs by the author.

Library of Congress Cataloging-in-Publication Data

Snyder, Tom, date
    Pacific Coast highway : traveler's guide / Tom Snyder.
        p.   cm.
    Includes index.
    ISBN 0-312-26370-8
    1. Pacific Coast Highway—Tours.   2. Pacific Coast (Wash.)—Tours.
3. Pacific Coast (Or.)—Tours.   4. Pacific Coast (Calif.)—Tours.   5. Automobile travel—Washington (State)—Guidebooks.   6. Automobile travel—Oregon—Guidebooks.   7. Automobile travel—California—Guidebooks.
I. Title.

F851.S715 2000
917.9504'44—dc21   00-027325

10   9   8   7   6   5   4

CONTENTS

ACKNOWLEDGMENTS

There are moments in life's journey that point us toward an unseen goal. In Laguna Beach, the owners of the Carousel, and the actress Miss Bette Davis, taught a gangly kid to see beyond the highway.

My heartfelt gratitude also goes to the professionals who helped this book come together. I especially want to thank Carol Lavender and Suzen Brasile, who started me off in the right direction. Many thanks as well to Jon Adler, Kristi Agren, Alisha Allen, Laurie Armstrong, Peggy and Ed Backholm, John Biord, Tia Bledsoe, Nancy Borino, Kathleen Boyle, Sara Bray, Mary Ann Carson, Mark Carter, John Daily, Lauren Ash Donohue, Chris Donovon, Jennifer Felice, Joe Finnie, Cynthia Fontayne, Leslee Gaul, Kathleen Gordon-Burke, Jeff Grover, Mandi Hagerman, Koleen Hamblin, Susan Hastings, Gale Hemmen, Colleen Henderson, Amanda Holder, Cindy Hu, Marcey Ivory, Maggie Ivy, Malei Jessee, Kelly Jones, Kathi Joy, Kim Kimball, Maria Kuhn, Steven Landy, Suzie Lankes, Tom Martin, Effie McDermott, Michal and Allan Miller, Cookie Mullineaux, Rebecca Pieken, Karen Runkel, Renee Rux, Fred Sater, Beve Saukko, Diane Schostak, Terry Selk, Kevin Shea, Ned Simmons, Tony Smithers, Linda Spaulding, Larry Stoffel, Joyce Webb, Susan Welty, and Gene Woodwick. You are all extraordinary.

Special thanks go to my editor, Julia Pastore, for her enthusiasm and wise counsel, and to Jim Powell—always ready for another road book—whose support and friendship is beyond measure.

YOUR PERSONAL TOUR

Highways can usually be driven in either direction, but books are pretty much a one-way proposition. So everything possible has been done to make this guide useful whether you are traveling north or south.

- A town-by-town narrative for the entire highway follows, with towns and special wayside areas printed in boldface type.
- Where directions are detailed, these are presented in boxes, for both northbound and southbound travelers.
- Alternate routes commonly used in case of storm or slide damage are covered as well.
- Special sections on books, food, and lodging are listed toward the back.

Which brings up the first major question: *In which direction is it best to drive the coast?*

To answer, you only need to know in what season you'll be traveling and how many days you have—the highway will tell you the rest.

In winter, the sun is lower on the horizon and not so intense, so driving toward it leads you into the warmth of Southern California. In summer, the cool forests of Oregon and Washington are inviting, so it feels good to put the sun over your shoulder and head north. But choose what feels best for you.

That's the major aim of this book, to be a traveling companion rather than a shop-here-eat-there guide.

Special places and attractions will be highlighted, but without laying out the journey in every detail. That way you'll be exploring your own possibilities, and the tour will be your adventure rather than someone else's.

Discounts, Maps, and Listings

Money-saving offers along PCH change daily and many disappear altogether during the summer. But one discount source you can count on every day is membership in the American Automobile Association.

Through the AAA's "Show Your Card and Save" program, you can expect discounts of 10 to 20 percent—enough to pay for your membership and realize some hefty travel savings, too. That's to say nothing of the value of a AAA card if you have a roadside emergency.

Cost of a one-year membership is around $40, varying from state to state, and members are entitled to free AAA TourGuides and maps for each state. Plus, if you are planning on doing much camping, the AAA publishes a comprehensive listing for California, Oregon, and Washington in their CampBook series.

NOTE: Other than state maps for California, Oregon, and Washington, there are exceptionally useful maps for your PCH tour. These include: San Diego Area, Oceanside-Escondido, Southern Orange County, Los Angeles—Southern Area, Los Angeles—Western. You'll also want the San Francisco city map. Free to members. Otherwise, $30 or more.

So if you're not already a member, do yourself a favor—and no, I don't get paid for saying this—by signing up with the American Automobile Association.

Seasonal Tips

If you hadn't guessed, the summer season in California coastal communities can range from bustling to jam-packed.

So if possible, plan your Pacific Coast Highway tour off peak-season. Labor Day to mid-June is best. One special inducement is that October to February is the season when Monarch butterflies return to California and can be found in abundance in Pacific Grove and a few choice eucalyptus groves along the coast. And, of course, the rates for lodging are invitingly lower.

Another advantage of traveling along the coast in the off-season—even by a few days or weeks—is that marginal operators, whose quality could not attract local business, are shuttered and gone. That makes finding a nice place to eat much easier.

If an off-season tour is unworkable, here are a few suggestions for making the most of your time along the coast.

- Make reservations well in advance in prime resort areas. And do all the information-gathering and booking you can over the Internet!
- Arrange overnight stays so you are *near* but not necessarily *in* a coastal resort city or other popular destination. Reservations will be easier to obtain and rooms less costly.
- If you are heading into a city like Los Angeles, time your arrival for about 9:30 A.M. and be clear of the freeways before 3:00 P.M. That will keep you out of the worst commuting traffic.

Information on attractions and accommodations is available from state departments of tourism and local visitors information centers. Promotional offers often accompany this material, so don't be shy.

PLANNING NOTE: For easy access to sources covering Pacific Coast Highway, visit **www.sentimental journeys.org.**

Making Your Tour Special

Now let's get to the fun part—planning your tour. For drivers from the East and airline passengers on direct flights, the major gateways to Pacific Coast Highway are Los Angeles and San Francisco.

Driving

The best corridors to follow driving out from the East are Route 66 and I-40, with I-10 as an alternative in the winter. Traveling Route 66 is always a joy, and takes six to ten days. (See *Route 66 Traveler's Guide and Roadside Companion* for details.) Best of all, a tour of Pacific Coast Highway will neatly cross the T of your Route 66 journey.

For a full tour of Pacific Coast Highway, San Diego makes the best beginning point. Starting from San Diego will require one to three days. If you haven't the time, turn north from Santa Monica for all but one hundred fifty miles of spectacular coastline.

In order not to feel rushed, figure on nine to ten days one-way for a full Pacific Coast tour. Allowing a little extra time for special places in each of the three states, it's best to plan on twelve to thirteen days to do the entire coast in one direction; at least three weeks overall.

Spectacular but shorter tours are also possible, but let's look at the full-course treatment first.

Complete Dream Tour
More of the West Coast can be explored with fly-drive-rail than any other way. If you are coming by air from the East or are taking an international flight, an all-pro dream tour can be yours by driving in one direction and returning via train to your arrival point. It's generally less expensive, too.

I've driven the West Coast, flown it at beach-house level, hitchhiked some of the highway, and ridden the rest on a motorcycle—probably in more than one incarnation—and I must tell you that the grandest complement to your drive is a return trip by rail through the Cascade Mountains. It will leave you breathless.

And as if that weren't enough, the Amtrak route along California's beaches will finish the job. For even though the coast highway is close to the ocean, the train offers a different and more intimate perspective.

If you are arriving at LAX, there are several options. You can pick up a rental car for the first leg south to San Diego. Or you might take Amtrak's marvelous Pacific Surfline service from Union Station in Los Angeles direct to city center in San Diego. Or, your airline may offer discount seating on connections from LAX.

The vehicle you choose will turn out to be a crucial decision, however. Make sure you choose something you'll enjoy driving and living with for your tour.

At Budget car rental you can even choose a Ford Ranger or a Mustang. Prefer a Jaguar? No problem. You could even request a real Woodie surfwagon—with Budget's huge fleet of fun cars, they might even have one. Not all specialty cars qualify for one-way rentals, though, so you may have some secondary choices to make.

A mid-sized car can be rented from Budget for twelve days with unlimited mileage for $300 to $500, depending on the season. And there is *no* drop-off charge. Specialty vehicles are in the $400 to $900 range. And your AAA card entitles you to a discount.

Other agencies offer similar rates, but you may encounter hefty one-way surcharges. As we go to press, Budget certainly looks like the best deal around. View their fleet at each location and make easy reservations online at www.budget.com. It's also wise to secure your rental early to take advantage of additional savings.

TRAVELER'S TIP: It is generally less expensive to rent through a hotel or downtown office during the week and at an airport on weekends. You may not always find the same selection of vehicles, though, so check on both.

Now, here comes the dream part. After you follow Pacific Coast Highway north, board Amtrak's classic Coast Starlight at Seattle or Olympia for your return through the Shasta Mountains to Los Angeles via Portland, the Bay Area, and Santa Barbara.

Travelers from the Northwest may board the train for the southern leg and return home by rental over Pacific Coast Highway.

NOTE: Don't confuse Coast Starlight service with southbound trains traversing California's central valley.

The Coast Starlight departs Seattle or Olympia before noon and you'll arrive in Los Angeles the next evening, refreshed and ready to head on home with stories of everything you've discovered on your journey.

A one-way coach reservation on Amtrak costs $120 to $170 (less if you are a student, senior, disabled, or a AAA member). You'll also be saving on accommodations, rental days, and fuel. Book via 1-800-USA-RAIL and receive a special rate with Hertz.

Shorter Dream Tours
Sometimes a split of champagne is just right for an early evening. And the same goes for touring. If you have fewer than ten days, take advantage of seasonal differences along the West Coast—make San Francisco your gateway.

In summer, take a cool, restful drive north from San Francisco, along unspoiled beaches in the Pacific Northwest and through the forests. You can walk for miles on parts of the coastline without seeing another soul. And just as the sea changes, each redwood and western cedar forest casts its own kind of enchantment. In three days you can make Portland; five will carry you around to Seattle.

At other times of the year, when the blahs set in, fly into San Francisco, rent a snappy little convertible, and head south along California's sun-drenched beaches. Again, except on weekends, you might have the whole place pretty much to yourself. With an overnight in Santa Cruz, three days will take you to Los Angeles; five will easily see you through to San Diego.

Whether north or south, though, combine your drive with Amtrak's superb Coast Starlight or Pacific Surfline service for return, or fly home from your final destination.

> You'll find information on a number of travel options at **www.sentimentaljourneys.org**, a site designed for travelers planning tours on Pacific Coast Highway, Route 66, and other two-lane highways across America.

Now, take a step back in time with me and imagine the West Coast as it was in the decades after the 1930s. That was the heyday of the highway you're about to travel.

What was playing on the radio? What were travelers' fears and dreams back then? What did they find along this very special highway? What will you find . . . ?

Retro-touring is about what Jack Kerouac called "the goingness of it all." It's also about fusing memories and stories of the past in order to enrich the present—bringing us more fully into each moment, producing a new level of experience.

Rain. Heat. An ice-cold drink. Stories of romance and adventure. Sunset colors. Nat King Cole. Garcia. The Beach Boys. A stranger's welcoming smile.

Traveling is also about the simple things in life, often lost in the shuffle of our regular world. On the road they become important again. So traveling is about being regular. It's about buying dopey T-shirts and sometimes acting silly for the camera. Traveling is about having a bathroom every day that is cleaner than the one at home.

And traveling is about knowing that you started your day way back *there* and ended up way over *here*.

LIFE AND TIMES OF PCH

The West Coast has miles of great highways. But the three states rarely agreed on signage, and California once created the most godawful numbering system of all. Pacific Coast Highway is heir to those inconsistencies, so here's a thumbnail history.

In 1909, the California State Legislature established numbered highways. These numbers were never posted along highways, but appeared on maps until 1958—at which time there were 240 such routes.

Later, in the mid-1920s, a new numbering system was developed for all U.S. highways. North-south routes were assigned odd numbers, and east-west routes were assigned even numbers. Another feature of the new numbering system was the practice of assigning the number 1 to north-south highways of importance. The easternmost road along the Atlantic Coast became US 1, and so on.

In the ensuing scramble, what was originally called Pacific Highway became US 99, while the north-south highway farther west became US 101.

That made sense at the time, but other interests were at work and optional routings of US 101 appeared, including: US 101E, US 101W, US 101A, and Bypass US 101. For a while, 101 was all over the place.

Worse, when transportation officials began numbering routes that had already been signed by the auto clubs, these numbers were different from the legislative numbers. Some routes actually had three separate numbers at the same time!

For example, the coastal highway from the junction of US 101 in Ventura County to Los Angeles—officially named Pacific Coast Highway—was also listed as Legislative Route 60, State Signed Route 1, and US 101A. And in Malibu, the road was for a time known as Roosevelt Highway. Near San Diego, it's now a county road. In the north, US 101 is signed as the Redwood Highway or Pacific Coast Scenic Byway.

So while the route in this guide is derived from the US 101 series, along with highways like CA 1, our test-travelers thought the term *Pacific Coast Highway* would be easiest for visitors to grasp, while a route closest to the ocean would be their preference.

And that's what we decided to do.

WOODIES, SURFING, AND LIFE

What's a Woodie? Well, for one thing a Woodie is the last remnant of the true coach-builders' art, dating from a time when wood was the structural material of wagons and early automobiles. Not stamped steel, covered with bits of stick-on plastic.

That much is history. But a Woodie is also an icon, emblematic of beaches and surfing and Pacific Coast Highway and much of what people who live along the ocean care about deeply.

Around 1910, automobiles were just going into serious production and companies were looking toward a vehicle that could replace the horse-drawn depot hacks that hauled passengers and their luggage from the railway depot to a local hotel.

It was a throwback, really. But even Henry Ford—not exactly a spendthrift—could see that customers treasured them. By the late 1920s, these depot hacks were being called estate wagons to help sell the idea to mansion-dwellers who had enough money to buy a high-ticket item.

People, then as now, fell in love with the retro look of the Woodie. But the vehicles still had no windows and were basically wagons with roofs and penny-ante engines.

By the late 1930s, Woodies had much of the look that we associate with them today. But there was a problem with owning a car built almost entirely of wood—maintenance. Early finishes did not hold up well in eastern winters or under western sun. And one by one, the wagons everyone loved were traded on the cheap for steel-bodied cars.

Many used Woodies turned up in Southern California,

where they were snapped up as luxury symbols in a land where you are what you drive.

Yet Woodies did little better in the damp, salt air, and one by one, they were resold—or given to do-nothing sons who spent their days at something called surfing.

It was then that the Woodie surf-wagon was born. Hundreds of them dotted the California coast in the 1950s and early '60s as surfing became popular. With international competition and media attention, early surfers grew toward godhood. Younger surfers and collectors were soon paying dearly for the old Woodies their heroes had been driving. And in that moment the Woodie passed into song and legend.

Today, surviving Woodies (now numbering only a fraction of the thousands built) recall sweet days of surf and sand and music and good times. What's even more important is that every Woodie reminds us that it was once a tree—and how fragile our connection is with the bounty on which the entire coast is founded.

Which brings us back to surfing and its relationship to life, along the waveline and elsewhere. For surfing offers a connection with nature and power—and one's own sweet juices—that few activities can match.

Airplanes and other high-performance machines are certainly thrilling, and there are few rushes equal to dialing a motorcycle up to a hundred and watching the world blur by. Yet it's all mechanical; even sky-diving is machine-dependent. Not surfing.

On the water, it is just you—a resin sliver under your toes—and tons of rolling sea water in a ten- or twenty-foot wave right over your shoulder. If you've never surfed, you can take it on faith that this is both a humbling and ecstatic experience.

As a result, surfers tend to hold great respect for the coastline and for the nature that created it. When I first began traveling this coast, it struck me as odd that the surf-buggies, whether at the beginning or end of the day, always seemed to be in the slow lane. I was not at peace with anything then; I didn't understand those who were.

As you cruise Pacific Coast Highway, today, on your own special journey, you might want to keep that in mind.

"Life," as John Lennon once said, "is what happens while you're making other plans."

READY FOR SOME SURFING OF YOUR OWN?

Since you'll be driving along many of the most famous surfing spots in the world, you might want to give it a shot. When you get home, you'll know what the words mean in the Beach Boys' "Surfin' Safari."

Following are suggestions for working your way into surfing as you travel. Surf shops are plentiful along the coast from Southern California to northern Washington. Nearly all rent equipment, provide lessons, and are glad to offer advice as well. They're veterans and can save you time and trouble. So don't be afraid to ask questions.

Most surfers will be happy that you're interested in a sport they've spent years mastering. However, with the rise in interest in surfing has come some new territoriality—localism. Know where you're welcome.

If you're really serious and will be spending more than a few days along the coast, hook up with a surfing school, if at all possible. The days are gone when the only way to learn was go out and let the board hit you in the head day after day. With lighter, quicker boards and leashes, it's much easier to get yourself into trouble.

Surfers vary in their ability on the water and at instruction. At a school, both experience and coaching ability are crucial, but if you must choose between the two, go for the coaching! And be absolutely sure you are comfortable with your instructor. It is not only your right to choose a teacher, it is your duty to yourself to choose well.

If you are a woman, be certain there are women instructors on staff—and that you get one. Distribution of weight and strength are entirely different for a woman, as is communication at the intuitive level. Might as well have all this working for you.

One last note: getting to a standing position is exciting, and some instructors go for that right away. But far more important is mastering fundamentals. Don't be hurried.

Here are a few schools to consider. They all provide

equipment and everything from group to individual rates—generally from $30 to $90 per two-hour session.

Kahuna Bob's Surf School covers the surfline from San Diego north through Leucadia and has been around a while. (Kahuna) Bob Edwards is also house surfing director at Hotel del Coronado, so if you're staying there, this is a convenient, and classy, place to start. (760-721-7700)

High marks for professionalism go to Pat Weber's **San Diego Surfing Academy.** And they're attuned to students' needs from remedial to putting boardroom executives on surfboards. (619-565-6892)

Pascowitz Surf Camp, based in San Clemente and operating at San Onofre, will accommodate individuals and small groups. Perhaps the most widely repected— and loved—of western surf schools, this has been a tradition for a well-known physician and his family for over twenty years. If you want an Aloha experience, this may be what you're looking for. (949-361-9283)

It's a Girl Thing Surf School in Santa Cruz is, by any measure, one of the best surfing schools to be found anywhere. And if you're a hairy-chested male, don't let the name put you off. These women are tops as surfers and as coaches. (831-462-5873)

Still, if you are a dedicated do-it-yourselfer, here's how you might work surf-learning into your travels along the coast.

Beginning in the south—where you won't need a wetsuit to stay warm—watch for beaches where there are plenty of swimmers and a lifeguard tower. That will usually keep you away from a rocky seafloor. Look for light surf that will break just above your waist. Practice diving through breaking waves, then move to chest-deep water outside the break and learn how to bob as waves move on past you. Coronado and La Jolla are usually good for this. Ocean Beach is a good place to begin noticing what the surfers are doing.

Continuing north, watch for beaches where swimmers are bodysurfing. San Clemente and Laguna are both pretty good. The Wedge at Newport is famous, but not a really good idea for novices.

Notice how bodysurfers duck through waves and bob until a good crest comes along, kicking and stroking to catch the leading edge. Their arms go to their sides in a classic Superman position, head up, chest forward in front of the break. Practice this in easy shoulder-high waves until your neck is sore, then call it a day.

By the time you're up to the beach cities, Redondo and Hermosa, start watching the kids on bodyboards. Bodyboards are around forty inches in length and a natural extension of bodysurfing, with a faster, longer ride. Practice steering by leaning and shifting your weight to go faster or slower.

Surf shops rent bodyboards. You can buy a used board or a new blem for under $100 and sell it later. Or you can pick up a cheap Boogie board in almost any supermarket near the beach. Just know that these break pretty easily under an adult.

By the time you reach Malibu and Ventura County line and Rincon, you will have had time to watch surfers working all kinds of waves and sets and breaks. There are plenty of surf shops all along these beaches, and you can catch a lesson or two with equipment included, and get accustomed to a wetsuit and a soft surfboard.

Santa Cruz is the last of the south-facing beaches and the perfect place to take a lesson or two that will stick with you farther north in Oregon and Washington.

Now let's head out. Surf's up!

PACIFIC COAST HIGHWAY PROJECT

When I wrote my first traveler's guide on Route 66 a few years ago, that once-great highway was being abandoned. I am happy to have been a part of a revival that has led over a quarter million travelers to rediscover the old highway. Yet for a time it was a close-run thing.

Happily, Pacific Coast Highway is in no such danger—unless we neglect the gorgeous beaches that embrace this grand roadway. Because if the waters continue to be polluted and the sand littered with personal refuse, PCH will not survive or flourish.

So this traveler's guide is a reference point for a larger vision. The California-Oregon-Washington coastline is a special heritage. What we do, or fail to do here, will affect not only our children, but generations to come. Nature is slow to be ruined—and slower still in recovery.

Consequently, a share of any royalties due me as the author will be donated to shoreline conservation groups.

Further, the Pacific Coast Highway Project will co-sponsor events designed to bring funds to the volunteer organizations struggling daily to keep the shoreline and coastal habitats as clean and sparkling as we know they can be.

If you would like to join in supporting this work, visit the **www.sentimentaljourneys.org** web site for up-to-date information on the project.

Or consider joining the Surfrider Foundation. For over fifteen years, this nonprofit organization has concentrated its efforts to preserve the world's oceans, waves, and beaches. With over forty-five grassroots chapters in the U.S. and four international affiliates, the world's coasts are safer from pollution. Visit them at www.surfrider.org for information or phone them (800-743-7873).

Meantime, as you travel one of the most beautiful highways in the world, remember to respect as well as enjoy these beaches. Give some thought to how long all this has taken to create, how it nurtures us. And how fragile we all are.

THE WEST COAST

California, Oregon, and Washington are very different in their viewpoints and cultures, but one thing unites the three states, and that is a common history of isolation from the rest of the country.

With the exception of automobiles, which were trucked west well into the 1950s, heavy items like appliances were built on the West Coast to avoid heavy eastern freight charges. In fact, it was not until the 1960s that Southern Pacific finally had a double-track system into California.

The Rocky Mountains and coastal ranges remain formidable barriers. Any map of the coastal region shows only a few north-south corridors and almost no east-west portals through the great mountain ranges. So except for a trickle of transcontinental traffic, the West Coast had to make do.

One example stands for all the rest. From 1904 through 1957, the Pacific Coast Baseball League was one of several minor leagues around the country, but it developed a style of play and a level of interaction with fans like no other.

Did you know that the record for the world's longest

home run was set by George McDonald of the San Diego Padres? (The Padres were formed in 1936 when the Hollywood Stars were moved south.) One day George knocked it clean out of the park. The ball took a helluva bounce off Pacific Coast Highway, flew into a boxcar—and ended up in L.A., 125 miles away! The event was duly recorded in *Ripley's Believe It or Not!*

Players were hometown boys who often gave up major league opportunities to stay with a local organization, inspiring great fan loyalty and intense rivalries between teams.

For decades PCL clubs met their schedules up and down the coast by train or bus, largely ignored by the rest of the country. That's because, until the early 1950s, big-league baseball was limited to only ten eastern cities in the U.S.

So the Pacific Coast League played on, dreaming of becoming a major league of its own. And why not? Minor-league clubs invented baseball under the lights and the system of post-season playoffs.

Instead, the roof fell in. The Brooklyn Dodgers moved to Los Angeles, and the Giants went to San Francisco, while television advertisers and viewers became baseball's market rather than ballpark regulars.

The old Pacific Coast League is gone now, steamrolled, like most things historic, by distant economic interests. Only the Tacoma Rainiers recall what was once a consuming passion on the West Coast.

The Portland Beavers and the Seattle Suds and the Oakland Oaks and the San Francisco Seals—in whose employ, Joe DiMaggio slammed his way to a sixty-one-game hitting streak during the 1933 season—all disappeared. Only through piety, perhaps, did the Padres and the Angels make it out alive.

What passes for the Pacific Coast League today has teams in places like Tennessee and Iowa. Arguably, the Osaka Buffaloes have a greater call on being in a Pacific Coast League than does Louisiana.

Has the demise of the old PCL ruined us all? Of course not. But it is a powerful reminder of the kind of homogenization that is abroad in the land. And a sweet remembrance of how it once was.

CALIFORNIA

Contradictions abound in California. There are so many, in fact, that they could make up the state flower. And the place is so big no one has a chance of figuring it all out. Of the 1,900 miles you'll be driving along the coast, over half will be in California. Yet unlike other large places, no two miles along California's coast are alike.

The same can be said for the state's society and politics. If New England invented Yankee disagreement, California has raised it to an art-form and in election years, a bloodsport.

Eugene Burdick once wrote that there were three Californias: north and south, plus the great central valley. But even that misses the mark in a place with so many cultures and subcultures, a place supported by economies as diverse as aerospace and the garment trade, computers, automotive design, tourism, and the movies.

The resulting California attitude is basically not to bother about having one. Which seems to annoy a lot of people from out-of-state. Some critics even point out that all of California is in denial about death from earthquakes, fires, and tsunamis. That's undoubtedly true. Of course, other parts of the country are in denial about life. Perhaps it all evens out.

Basically, Californians seem to be saying, "Jeez, we got sun and ocean and wilderness and great skiing and enchanted islands offshore, what's to get bothered about?" Exactly.

Still, the contradictions persist. On the surface California is viewed as falling-down liberal. Nothing could be further from the truth. To be sure, most of the state is vegetarian-friendly. And there are indeed clothing-optional beaches, but very few compared to Europe and none at all in gigantic Los Angeles County.

Most everything in the crowded southern part of California is buttoned down tight. Remember, this is the state in which Earl Warren (later the target of impeachment billboards in Orange County) signed an order imprisoning thousands of loyal Japanese-American families—costing them their homes, businesses, land, and honor. And it was at the garden clubs of Glendale that Ronald Reagan got his political start. Nixon was a local boy as well. So when it comes to retrograde conservatism, California's credentials are undeniable.

Yet for all its peculiarities of deed and belief, parts of California are still close to paradise. And those are the places we're headed for. But not by freeway, not by those mega-highways that carry 250,000 vehicles a day. Whew.

Instead we'll be taking meandering two-lane and county roads, generally as close to the shoreline as possible. For even though coastal cities can be crowded, they reflect the ocean by remaining least changed over the decades.

There's something about getting your feet into the sand or your body into a wave that keeps everything in perspective. Beach regulars, whose clock is the sun, and surfers, whose biorhythms match the waves, may be the wiser. No nine-to-five stress there.

The film *Lifeguard* and the Beach Boys hymn "Let's Get Together and Do It Again" say it all pretty well. If the sense of a life well lived has escaped you recently, check these out. And carry their poignant sweetness with you as we go in search of an older, more amiable California along Pacific Coast Highway.

Southern Coast

This part of the state is under constant reconstruction. Economic pressure on the land is enormous and buildings here often last for only a couple of decades, which gives Southern California such a contemporary, glassed-in look that much of it looks as though it has simply spilled over from Disney's Tomorrowland.

California is typically divided into north and south along a line centered roughly on Fresno. People along the coast think that's silly and they're right. So we'll consider the southern part of the state as extending from San Diego north through Malibu.

SAN DIEGO AREA

Often thought of as California's Other City, **San Diego** is second in size only to Los Angeles, with better weather and fewer earthquakes than almost anybody. San Diego is rarely mentioned in the same breath as San Francisco (what is?) or even Santa Barbara.

Yet San Diego is a rich and vibrant city, with marvelous places to hang out or hide out, plus world-class attractions. It deserves a wider reputation and more visitors bent on discovering the city's gifts. Because this is an absolutely marvelous place.

PLANNING NOTE: San Diego has so much to offer, even regular visitors are boggled. So call for the "Official Visitors Planning Guide," published by the San Diego Convention and Visitors Bureau. (619-236-1212)

Also, check with the International Visitors Information Center at 11 Horton Plaza, on the First Avenue side, at F Street, as soon as you hit town. They can assist you in selecting lodgings and restaurants from the bewildering range, and guide you in lower-cost ticket purchases for local attractions.

As a thumbnail: San Diego Mission was the first of those founded by Junipero Serra and carries an almost palpable feeling of history. John Montgomery was experimenting with unpowered flight here almost a decade before anyone else, and Charles Lindbergh's *Spirit of St. Louis* was built by fledgling Ryan Aircraft. And with the U.S. Navy a major player here, it was natural that San Diego became a center for aviation. During the 1950s and '60s, however, the city suffered from the boom-and-bust cycle of military spending, and has only recently stabilized its economy on a long-term basis.

Despite all that, San Diego has always retained the home-town feel of a city that works. So there is no better place to begin or end your journey than San Diego—and none more romantic than the Hotel del Coronado on **Coronado Island.**

A national icon for over a hundred years, the Del is one of the last remaining examples from the Queen Anne Revival period, and certainly the finest. And that's only the beginning. If hotel ratings were awarded for history, timeless design, climate, and sheer charm, the Del would be a ten-star hotel, and deserving of every one of them.

The hotel is also the largest and most beautiful Woodie imaginable. Built entirely from lumber shipped in from the Pacific Northwest in 1888, the structure is a tribute to what can be done when we don't think about something too much, but simply do it. The Del was being designed while construction proceeded. That's a book in itself.

Here we must be content with saying that if you stay at no other top-drawer hotel on your journey along America's West Coast, make it the Del. Rooms range from about $200 on up to $2,300 for the Beach House—which is always booked. The hotel is a mythical place, with its roster of kings and presidents, movie stars, and yes, even a resident ghost. (619-435-6611)

As spiritual signatures go, rooms 3502 and 3312 register more clearly than most. Guests and employees have reported footsteps, breezes occurring when windows are tightly closed, unexplained voices, and other supernatural phenomena for decades. All this activity began with the death of lovely Kate Morgan, quite possibly at her husband's hand, back in 1892.

Tom Morgan was known as a gambler and all-around cad during the time he and Kate traveled together. But when his wife became pregnant, Tom's anger surfaced; the two separated and Kate took up residence at the Del. Not long after, her body was found on the beach, a pistol beside her. Following the funeral, her maid at the hotel disappeared, because, many believe, she had witnessed a murder.

Whatever the source of activity in the Del's two rooms, both story and ghost continue to be updated. New clues are sometimes found in old accounts—and if Kate's ghost is resident, she has also learned to turn the television set on and off by herself.

On a far more material plane, *Some Like It Hot,* with Marilyn Monroe, was filmed here, together with *The Stunt Man,* an outrageous dark comedy, featuring Peter O'Toole and the Del's parapets. Also—as you'll be reminded from time to time—many of the jet-action scenes in *Top Gun,* with Tom Cruise and Kelly McGillis, were shot right next door at North Island Naval Air Station and aboard USS *Ranger.*

If you are unable to stay at the Del, be sure to take the marvelous heritage tour offered by the hotel ($15), and visit the free History Gallery on the lower Galleria level, with twenty-seven displays of timeless photos and artifacts. Then, if you are still short of time, look briefly through the shop, Est. 1888, and grab a take-out at the Del Deli.

Each moment spent in the hotel or on the grounds will bring you closer to the essence of what has always been most enchanting about Southern California.

> To reach Hotel del Coronado easily, transition from I-5 in San Diego to SR 75 over the toll bridge to Coronado Island. Turn left on Orange Ave., continue six blocks and bend left to the hotel at 1500 Orange Ave. Avoid Coronado's streets around three on weekday afternoons, however, when a mob of workers from North Island NAS all head for home.

Other points of special interest are neatly arranged along a circular route from Loma Light to the downtown waterfront.

Of all the places to visit in San Diego, Loma Light at Cabrillo National Monument is one best done early, so you may want to begin there. Gates open at 9 A.M.

Surrounding Cabrillo National Monument are pre–World War II fortifications that are endlessly fascinating to both adults and children. After Pearl Harbor, this country came perilously close to defending itself on California's beaches, and right here is where the toughest fight would have been, with San Diego and its premier naval installations as the prize.

> From Point Loma, return via Cabrillo Memorial Dr. and Catalina Blvd. Angle right on CA 209. Follow the bend through to a left turn and continue north on Rosecrans St. and Taylor St. to Old Town.

If you're interested in the cultural roots of California or in searching out old highway alignments, you'll want to check out Old Town. Old Pacific Coast Highway went right through it, and much of the color of the day has been preserved here.

And about six miles northeast of Old Town, via I-8 and I-15, at 10818 San Diego Mission Road, stands Basilica San Diego De Alcala. If you are planning to visit many of the California missions, this is a natural, if often overlooked, starting point. The structure itself was moved from its original location some time ago, the Franciscans being very high on adaptive reuse, to a site with better water and soil.

San Diego Mission also gave California its first martyr, Frey Luis Jaime, who confronted a rampaging mob with simple words of love and was slaughtered for his trouble.

Now your history teachers, and probably your mother, would vote to visit Old Town and the mission. But if you have only one day in San Diego, I'd beat it on out to Belmont Park at Mission Beach.

There you'll find one of the last two Woodie roller-coasters on the West Coast—the other is in Santa Cruz—and it's a beauty. Plus there's a carousel that's just wonderful. Ostriches and wild beings of all kinds circle to the beat along with the horses. And on the way you'll be driving the beautiful Sunset Cliffs.

> To reach Belmont Park from Point Loma, return via Cabrillo Memorial Dr. and Catalina Blvd. to Hill St., just short of Point Loma Park. Turn left on Hill and take it to the end of the line, turning right on Sunset Cliffs Dr. Continue to a transition onto Mission Bay Blvd. and follow the signs to Mission Beach–Belmont Park

If you'd like to check out the surfing scene and Dead Head shops, turn onto very cool Newport Avenue in Ocean Beach.

From Belmont Park, it's a splendid drive through ivy-covered roadway arches to Balboa Park, a Disneyland for both mind and senses, that history teachers, nuns, and jet jockeys alike will love. But be forewarned—you could spend a week here without repeating anything. So do a little homework first—so you'll know something of how this amazing park came to be—and have a little touring plan in mind.

> From Belmont Park, return via Mission Bay Blvd. to I-8, transition to I-5 southbound and exit at Park Blvd. Signs for the San Diego Zoo will get you there as well.

The mechanically driven among us will want to turn left on President's Way for the San Diego Aerospace Museum and the San Diego Automotive Museum. Housed in the building Henry Ford commissioned for the 1935 exposition, the aerospace collection of sixty-five vintage aircraft, plus over seven hundred scale models, is just stunning—ranging from a replica of Lindbergh's Ryan to a very rare Japanese Zero, salvaged from the bottom of the Pacific, requiring 11,000 hours to restore.

No less surprising is the automotive collection, which includes Hudsons, Gable Cars, Deusenbergs, '60s musclecars—the Route 66 exhibit—town cars, Indy machines, and one of the very rare Tucker Torpedos. They're all here—and all cherry. Which is to say nothing of the rare Indians, Harleys, and other bikes on display.

A pleasant walk farther north in the park, past the

Japanese Friendship Garden and the Spreckels Organ Pavilion, will put you close to the Ruben H. Fleet building, which houses an Omnimax theater, plus a number of space exhibits, and the Model Railroad Museum, located in the lower level of Casa de Balboa.

If you're a train buff, ever had a toy train, or ever wanted one, this is a must-do. The museum houses the world's largest model railroad with awesome rolling stock, trestles, and yards. And there's a toy train layout where kids and adults blow whistles and run trains to their hearts' content.

For decades, however, the San Diego Zoo has been the true star of Balboa Park. Setting the trend for all the wild-animal parks that have since been developed, the San Diego Zoo is still in its prime, and a wonderful tour for everyone.

Most exhibits in the park will be open by 10 A.M. and admission ranges from $3 to $12 for adults, less for kids and seniors.

Head back down Park Boulevard, turn right on Broadway and right again on Harbor Drive for a meal at one of the Embarcadero's excellent restaurants, and stroll on over to the Maritime Museum and *Star of India,* launched in 1863 and the world's oldest active ship.

Surviving collisions, cyclones, and mutinies, the iron-hulled beauty was brought here in 1926, and has been wowing visitors ever since. Do go aboard, and ask yourself: How is it that this iron hull, immersed in seawater for almost one hundred fifty years, hasn't turned into a pile of rusty flakes? There's a fascinating answer belowdecks.

The U.S. Navy has been in these waters for a while, too, and is a strong presence all along the West Coast. It has sometimes been an uneasy relationship, especially during the 1940s, when the navy pretty much *was* the West Coast. In fact, there are so many PCH stories (and movies) in which the navy plays a major role, that you might want to learn more firsthand.

The navy offers tours on Saturdays and Sundays of ships in port. There is no charge for admission, just check in at the Naval Station's main gate on Harbor Drive any time from 1 to 4 P.M.

Departing San Diego on I-5, exit at Grand Avenue

westbound, north of Mission Bay, and continue to the end and make a right on Mission, finally angling right onto Prospect Street, for a visit to **La Jolla** (*La-hoy-ya*).

This small but exclusive city—enclave, really, since it has always remained separate from San Diego—seems to have been tucked away in grandma's trunk for fifty years. Here and there the marks of time are visible, but for the most part La Jolla has managed to remain quaint and charming.

Because La Jolla has always attracted the rich and famous, people-watching in the town, by locals and visitors alike, has been raised to an art-form. At famed La Jolla Cove, for example, you don't even need to go to the beach to watch people on the beach. There has always been a fine gallery just above for first-class spectating.

Photographs taken around La Jolla Cove during the 1930s could, except for string bikinis and automotive grillework, be mistaken for last week's snapshots, such is the timelessness of this area.

But of all the special places here with roots deep in California's Golden Age, La Valencia Hotel is perhaps the most memorable. The history of this hotel, from its opening in 1926, has been closely intertwined with the leisurely pace of La Jolla itself.

During the 1920s, '30s, and '40s, stars came in droves. Chaplin and Garbo, Mary Pickford, Groucho. Later, Gregory Peck, Dorothy McGuire, and Mel Ferrer founded a summer playhouse to rival Pasadena's. La Valencia served them all. Discreetly.

For if movie stars and other notables stay at the Del, or Beverly Hills Hotel, or the Mark Hopkins, it is to be *seen* at play. Not so the little hideaways like La Jolla. In such places, the famous want to be recognized but not noticed. That's an odd little quirk of movie stars. They depend upon and need daily recognition, yet they wish to be treated just like everybody else—so long as that treatment is preferential.

And treating guests as if each one is special, while making no fuss about it, is the stock in trade of La Jolla and La Valencia. In turn, regular guests of the hotel embrace it with a fierce loyalty that, as often as not, precludes change.

Which is all to the good, for the whimsical accoutrements of La Valencia are part of its heritage.

There are the murals in the Whaling Bar —which were intended to be regularly repainted—and which no one now dares change. Or the floor-numbering system. Three stories extend below the lobby at 1132 Prospect Street. So would the lobby be on the first or the fourth floor? Neither, actually. Since three additional lower levels were originally planned, the lobby is on the seventh floor. A manager once tried to change that; the guests wouldn't let him.

In the 1950s, as the Korean War came to an end and hard times came to the area, only La Valencia maintained a vision for itself, and in large measure, it is responsible for La Jolla's character and position today.

La Valencia is a California classic, with rates from $230 to $550 (619-454-0771). If your schedule does not permit a stay this time, stop in for lunch or an evening drink in the Whaling Bar & Grill. And when you do, notice the streetlamp just a few feet to the left of the lobby entrance. It hasn't changed either—been there since 1928.

Continue west on Prospect Street and turn left on Torrey Pines Drive, then left again on La Jolla Shores Drive. This will take you down the old coast road and past the Birch Aquarium at Scripps. Continue left on Torrey Pines Road (S21). After Gennesee and Scripps Clinic, take the next exit onto the old road to the left, through Torrey Pines State Reserve.

There is magic in these rough-skinned old pines, and in the roadway that winds down among them. For Torrey Pines was once the location of one of the most exciting and prestigious road-racing events on the West Coast. For regular entertainment the locals used a huge cable-wound launcher to fling themselves into the air aboard sailplanes, to ride the wavefront along these bluffs—all within a few yards of the cliff faces.

But it was a chinos-and-polo-shirt thing. No one would have worn fluorescent outfits or called any of this *extreme sports*. Drivers and pilots showed up to have a little fun on weekends, with precious little ego involved.

As you drive through Torrey Pines State Park, on the old road, you'll be covering some of the same ground the racers did, and along the cliffs, radio-controlled models are still flown on the same wind, sometimes by some of those pilots, now aging, but with the same true hands.

A remaining piece of old 101A is visible just north of Solamar Drive. Notice how closely the highway followed the shoreline then—and still does today.

Most of the old 1930s concrete is buried under a coat of asphalt now, but just a few years ago it was still possible to drive along this section, listen to the cloppety-clop of expansion cracks under the tires, and recall sleepy Southern California in the '40s—just before the state became a star.

Here, you could turn off the roadway onto a sandy shoulder, pull your shoes off, and wade straight out into the Pacific just yards away. No parking hassles, no fees. Just grab a beach towel and find that perfect spot on the sand.

Happily, several of these People's Beaches still survive. But plan to be there before midmorning, especially in summer. Locals stake out early claims.

Northbound	Southbound
Watch for the beaches as you come down the hill. Continue to the next intersection and return on the ocean side of the road. Do not attempt a left- or U-turn near a parking area.	Down the hill from Solamar Dr., you'll find beach areas right along the highway. But watch for cars backing onto the highway or turning left across traffic from the northbound lane.

DEL MAR–CARLSBAD

If La Jolla has a history of being leisurely, Del Mar has been on the fast track for some time—ever since Bing Crosby and Pat O'Brien brought thoroughbred racing to the one-mile track at Del Mar Fairgrounds in 1937. Several boomlets had favored the town since it began as a hopeful resort in 1885, but it was really the thoroughbred club and the wealth it attracted that put this small city of five thousand on the map. Soon, everyone was coming to the racecourse here, even J. Edgar Hoover, though we're told he did not arrive in drag.

Today, the city has reached nearly a perfect balance between conservationists, which forced I-5 inland, and the kind of development represented by the lovely L'Auberge Hotel and the well-designed Del Mar Plaza. Residents here know that when a town has two miles of seacoast to work with, every shovelful of dirt counts.

So as you drive through Del Mar, with its unstressed, neo-revival look, keep the image in your mind and heart, and when we find coastal towns that have trashed themselves farther north, remember that could have happened here, too. And didn't.

North from the rarefied air of La Jolla and Del Mar, the beach cities are a reminder that money ain't necessarily it after all.

In **Solana Beach,** the meeting of sea and sand comes back into foreground. Surfing, bodyboarding, walking— none of these require oodles of cash or credit. Nor does talent and community fellowship. Check out the crafts-people, coffeehouses, shops, and restaurants in the Cedros Design District.

Cardiff-by-the-Sea is equally charming, as is **Leucadia,** with just the right amount of slack for beach towns. It is a friendlier life here, and if not more tranquil on days when the surf is up, it is certainly more peaceful. If you're pretty well wound up from what you do every day, and want a strip of coastline to unwind on, these towns—now all part of Encinitas—are about the best places in Southern California. Instead of the second hand, people here keep track of the hour hand. Well, sometimes.

Encinitas has, in addition to some of the best surfing around, hundreds of acres of flowers—twenty nurseries in all—that keep the rolling hills between here and Carlsbad alive with color, virtually year-round.

If flower power wasn't invented here in the 1960s, it could have been. There are enough blooms here to fill every rifle barrel in the world, and still send a bouquet to your sweetie. It is such a sight that the Highway Patrol warns travelers not to stop on the interstate to take photographs. From the air, the view is simply spectacular (see *Above the Coast*).

And as if that weren't enough, Encinitas is the site of Wavecrest, the annual event that draws some three hundred Woodies here to Moonlight Beach. To their everlasting credit, Wavecrest organizers permit no vendors on site. It really is all for fun.

Carlsbad is a city in transition. Long known as the "Village by the Sea," Carlsbad grew from a discovery of mineral waters that matched those found in Karlsbad, Bohemia. Since then the town has also been blessed in part by being a bit too far from both L.A. and San Diego. That has helped preserve the European village look of this charming town, where you can walk from the beach to almost anywhere.

Now, Legoland has set up shop here as well, making Carlsbad a solid destination point for families. So far it has been a good mix, and a boost for the many fine restaurants and shops in town.

A lovely old Victorian-style depot houses a visitor's information center, just a block east of the highway on Carlsbad Village Drive.

OCEANSIDE–SAN CLEMENTE

Right across the bridge from Carlsbad is **Oceanside.** But ask most Southern Californians about the town, and its burly neighbor Camp Pendleton will figure in the answer. Not much loss to Oceanside, which is getting along quite nicely, thank you very much. But travelers are missing out by not spending time here. Oceanside is a highway town, in the Route 66 tradition, and a beach town as well. Certainly works for me.

Community leaders are involved with the recent historic designation of US 101, as well they might be. The highway has been a continuing presence here that equals or exceeds the long-term cultural impact of the huge base to the north. US 101 arrived in 1925; the marines didn't land until 1942.

And Oceanside is beginning to take restoration and adaptive reuse seriously. The Star Theater, a classic movie house dating from 1958, has been completely restored, adding its neon glow to the night sky at 402 N. Coast Highway. A couple of blocks farther south is the California Surf Museum, an ably run museum with rotating exhibits, each honoring a surfing pioneer. Great stuff and worth a look, whether you're a regular dude or new to the sport.

On Coast Highway at Wisconsin, the 101 Cafe is both a local icon and a genuine road-food place where travelers can still get breakfast any time of day. The 101 Cafe began as a diner in 1928—the counters are where the old dining room was—and passed through several incarnations before being returned to its original name and purpose by the present owner, providing good food and friendly service, plus a dollop of history, to travelers along the coast. Stop in for a bit of both. The owner published a brief history of the 101 Cafe, plus a self-guided walking tour of Oceanside.

At the north end of The Strand you'll find one of those little curiosities from California's past. Built in 1928, the salmon-bright cottages were originally rentals. In the 1950s, they were finally sold as individual units. For under $6,000 each.

And at the intersection of Coast Highway and Mission Avenue stood another curiosity. Back when the auto club was responsible for roadway signing, they had placed a huge concrete signpost at a busy intersection in Los Angeles—where cars promptly began running into it.

So with a wisdom unique to the Automobile Club of Southern California, it was moved down to Oceanside—where cars promptly began running into it. A red light was installed to warn drivers, but that only distracted the unwary, who ran into the sign while wondering what the light was for. The sign was eventually scrapped, but not before making an impression on drivers and their vehicles hereabouts.

North of town you're obliged to take I-5 across Camp Pendleton—watch for slowing vehicles (and sometimes running people) at the Border Patrol blockade—but before getting tangled up in all that, take a loop through the Oceanside everyone on the interstate will miss.

32 CALIFORNIA

Northbound	Southbound
From Coast Hwy. at the US 101 Cafe, turn left on Wisconsin Ave. and right on The Strand for a cruise along the beach. Continue past Mission Ave. and turn right on Windward Wy. and back onto Coast Hwy.	From Coast Hwy., at Windward Wy., just past Neptune Wy., turn right and then left on The Strand for a cruise along the beach. Continue past Mission Ave. and turn left on Wisconsin Ave. to return to Coast Hwy.

The town of **San Clemente** has often been, as musicians are fond of saying, "between gigs," with its own boom-and-bust cycles. In the beginning, a man named Ole Hanson had a dream. He saw on this lovely bit of coastline a village done in Mission Revival style. Not only that, but the streets would be laid out just so, there would be a community center right from the start—not as an afterthought—and each owner would be a shareholder in the beach.

Well, you can imagine how that idea went over in real-estate crazy California, where everyone was in it for the fast buck, and towns simply grew like Topsy. Of course, it didn't all work out just the way Ole had dreamed it, but not far off. As you drive through San Clemente, notice how wide the streets are and how curiously it all seems to blend together over the land.

Somehow, through real estate booms and crashes, as Laguna Beach development crept farther south, San Clemente retained its drowsy character. Until the late 1960s.

Enter President Nixon's choice to locate his "Western White House" in San Clemente. With all the administration's to-and-fro from Washington, the town was soon awash with Secret Service types, the media, and assorted hangers-on.

San Clemente was suddenly on the map. And despite questions about how the presidential property was acquired, and the inconvenience to locals, the boom was welcomed by many and looked as though it would be a very long-term thing.

Enter Watergate and the grinding self-destruction of a man and his presidency. Suddenly San Clemente was struggling, and is still trying to recover from the blight of properties abandoned along the Coast Highway. The theater is closed, along with restaurants and other businesses built at the peak of a political boomlet.

There are lessons perhaps, about the wisdom of depending upon political winds blowing in Washington a continent away. Meantime, San Clemente is redefining itself in terms of what has been its closet industry—*surfing*.

In the face of long-time dominance by Huntington Beach and Hermosa and Santa Cruz, San Clemente has quietly become a surfing capital in its own right. Beginning with the San Onofre Surf Club, the oldest and largest in the world, San Clemente is home to five of surfing's leading publications, a half-dozen surf schools, and more professional surfers and champions than any other community. The champion Surfrider Foundation is headquartered here as well, working through a membership of 25,000, to create and maintain clean beach habitats and safe conditions for surfers and nonsurfers alike worldwide. And where a surf shop or two can be found in many villages of equal size, San Clemente has a dozen. Down here, the surf's *way* up.

At 450 N. El Camino Real, San Clemente has also established one of the most eclectic and elegant small museums you'll discover anywhere. For most travelers with some curiosity about the Nixon years, the Heritage Foundation presents a far more approachable side of the president.

Add to that photographs and remembrances of San Clemente's early years, Ole Hanson's dream, a nod to the U.S. Marine Corps, legends of surfing, plus a gallery of local artists, and you have a sweeping exhibit for a town this size. The Heritage Foundation is open every morning by 10 A.M. and, for a cultural overview of this part of the coast, is unbeatable.

DANA POINT–LAGUNA BEACH

Charm along this part of the Southern California coast is endemic, of course, and **Dana Point** is not without its own.

The town is named for Richard Henry Dana, author of *Two Years before the Mast*—which has not been out of print in over one hundred sixty years. A well-to-do student at

Harvard, Dana's health and eyesight failed, and he took the sea-cure.

Except, instead of going as a passenger, Dana signed on as one of the *Pilgrim*'s common seamen (who lived in the fo'c'sle up forward; hence, "before the mast") and after reaching California, was put to work throwing tanned hides off the bluff to waiting boats below. A remarkable sculpture by Benedict Coleman graces that spot.

Dana, well recovered, not only wrote his story, but finished Harvard Law, becoming a world authority on sea law—and not forgetting his own experience, a champion of seamen's rights.

There's a nice drive through town, which also passes the site of all that hide-throwing.

Northbound	Southbound
From CA 1, at the north end of Doheny Beach, after the bridge, turn left on Harbor Dr. and continue past the Embarcadero, as the street becomes Dana Point. At Scenic Dr., turn left. Continue on Strand and Selva. Turn left onto CA 1.	From CA 1, a few blocks south of Marmara, turn right on Selva Rd. and continue on Scenic Dr. At the next opportunity, turn right on Dana Point. Continue onto Harbor Dr. and turn right onto CA 1.

Today's Dana Point includes Capistrano Beach and Monarch Beach as well. The town has a fine yacht basin and hosts the Dana Point Marine Refuge, stretching west around the headlands from the harbor.

But the bluffs themselves are largely as Richard Henry Dana saw them in the 1830s. Headlands like these are commonly found in earthquake-prone areas, and you'll see similar forms in Mendocino, farther north.

Dana Point is a bustling tourist center, but retains the quaint look and feel of the small coastal town it once was.

If there is a ziggurat, a hierarchy of beach towns in California, **Laguna Beach** stands at the peak. This once-tiny and most beautiful artist's colony has accepted growth as a natural consequence of its location, but in a leisurely way, as it does everything else.

The result is that along the highway Laguna looks very much as it did in the 1940s and early '50s: splendid but exquisitely laid-back, warm but not overly welcoming. You make your own way here. The town is very clear about that. Pronouncements that you'd love to live here will be met with nods—locals understand what you are saying—but with very thin smiles. Enough people live here already.

There are exceptions, of course, and one was Laguna's unofficial Greeter. Regardless of wind, fog, or rain, Eiler Larsen stood daily in the same spot and waved to each person in every southbound car.

To the obvious discomfort of some, Larsen would lower his great, shaggy head to peer closely into a car and make direct eye contact. Almost no one slipped by unnoticed, even though it must have worn his arms out when the highway filled to capacity during the summer months.

But it was Eiler Larsen's divine purpose to say hello in the best way he could to all fellow human beings who found their way to his town, and he did so well that his place at the edge of the highway is called Greeter's Corner. There's a café there that serves a seafood taco that'll really get your surfin' knobs up.

Shops in town are, as always, terrific and there are plenty of art galleries. If you have specific tastes, check in at the very fine Laguna Art Museum first (they're even online with a newsletter) to save yourself time.

One type of gallery you won't see everywhere is Aviation Arts Gallery at 533 S. Coast Highway. Otherwise Laguna is the place to pick up that little seascape you've always wanted.

Main Beach in town is a great place to do people-watching, and not a bad bodysurfing beach. If you're a cove-person, however, there are several north of town where there often seems to be no one at all. Beach Access signs will guide you.

CORONA DEL MAR–LONG BEACH

South of Newport Beach, **Corona Del Mar** basked in the sun for decades, a wide spot in the road. A very good hamburger stand, and a gorgeous sweep of beach. A nice place to sit and watch surfers shred a few waves. But **Newport Beach,** immediately to the north, is the high-stakes player around here and real-estate overflow has largely made Corona Del Mar a suburb.

Indeed, if Beverly Hills had a beach, it would have

called itself Newport. The town enjoys a hyper-luxurious lifestyle, and has more yachts per capita than any place on the West Coast. If you are living at that level, Newport Beach has much to offer. If not, it's better if the lights on PCH are green. A bit of trivia makes the point: if Orange County, of which Newport Beach is the unofficial capital, were a nation, it would rank about thirtieth in the world for sheer wealth.

Huntington Harbor and Seal Beach are both isolated by rivers and marshlands, and **Huntington Beach,** no small beach community, but a major city, is next. Although you'll get some arguments in Santa Cruz and San Clemente, Huntington is known as the place where Hawaiian surfing came for a visit decades ago—and stayed.

Unless you are really pressed for time, take a break, a stroll, a meal at Duke's on Huntington Pier. Basically an upscale Surf-and-Woodie joint, Duke's (named for Duke Kahanamoku, the worldwide ambassador of surfing from the 1900s until his death in 1968) is still a great place to do lunch.

And just across from the pier, at 411 Olive Avenue, is the International Surfing Museum, where the legends of both surfing and surf culture are center stage, and memories lurk in every corner. Items associated with Duke are here, along with the camera Bruce Brown used for *Endless Summer.* If you're making anything like a surfing pilgrimage along Pacific Coast Highway, don't miss this collection. Open noon to five P.M.

The 1930s and '40s still live here as well, in an area of dowdy beach places now headed upscale: a fine old residence, parsed out into rentals but well-maintained and perfectly cast as "Wuthering Heights." And the bars—most with sea-deco portholes—recall days in the '40s and '50s, when canary yellow convertibles and white, dime-store yachting caps ruled the highway and could guarantee company for the evening.

Strip-mall signs pretty well rule the highway now. Today's winning entry is: *Karate Cleaners.* Certainly makes you want to stand well clear of any dirt, doesn't it?

If it's lunchtime, there's a Ruby's on the ocean side of

the highway south of Avocado. Sure, it's a chain, but the setting is nearly perfect for beach-diner modern.

Northbound	Southbound
Continue on CA 1 through Seal Beach and turn left on Westminster Blvd. through Naples and Belmont Shore. Right onto Ocean Blvd. again.	From Ocean Blvd. in Long Beach, angle left on Westminster Blvd. and continue through Belmont Shore and Naples. Turn right on CA 1 to Seal Beach.

Virtually an island in Alamitos Bay, **Naples** and its cousin, **Belmont Shore,** are two of the most charming neighborhoods to be found in the L.A. area. There is a small-town feeling about the streets and storefronts, and the mall-builders have not been allowed much access.

It's a nice place to take a break from the car, stroll a little, and let the neighborhood take you in. Naples even has an island within the island, modeled (far more successfully) on the canals of Venice, California. At Christmastime, the local boaters' Parade of Lights is one of the most beautiful of any in the Los Angeles area.

Entering the **Long Beach** area from the south along wide Long Beach Boulevard, the architecture gives new meaning to the word *eclectic.* Here, you'll find Mediterranean villas alongside California Craftsman style homes, with scattered bits of stucco to remind this gentried boulevard that it is still right across from the beach. Few places around Los Angeles echo the 1920s and '30s so well.

And a major attraction fits perfectly with that mood: the *Queen Mary,* south across Queensway Bridge from Ocean Boulevard at Magnolia. Once called a folly, the grand old Cunard liner was brought to Long Beach at a time when tourism wasn't all that hot and the city needed a boost.

Many said, of course, that the *QM* was not exactly the boost they had in mind. Since then the liner has become one of the great tourist attractions of Southern California, ranking with Disneyland and Universal Studios. Not bad, for a foolish idea.

Part of the *Poseidon Adventure,* a watery disaster film in the *Airport* tradition, plus any number of television shows, were filmed here on the *QM,* which features both guided and self-guided tours.

LOS ANGELES

Often cast as a collection of suburbs in search of a city, L.A. has been overmaligned. Of course, it is true to some extent—there are eighty-eight cities in the **Los Angeles** metropolitan area, spread over two thousand square miles.

But the old inter-city rivalries are changing. Even as areas from the barrios to beach cities strengthen their own identities, and the San Fernando Valley is headed for independence, the metropolitan area is coming together in ways not seen before.

Some say it's too late; others claim it's just in time. Probably it's a little of both. Still, if one human being is relatively unpredictable, 8.5 million of them are going to be full of surprises.

Crossing L.A. (*AL-ay* or *EL-ay,* depending on your neighborhood) is a daunting prospect at any time of day. Before 9:30 in the morning and after 3:00 in the afternoon, traffic moves at just a little more than zero miles an hour. Sometimes less. Cars from all two thousand square miles of L.A. want to use the same freeway lanes at the same time.

So we'll be taking a route closest to the sea, which will be better for your lungs and a lot easier on your nerves. Cooler, too, if you are traveling in the summer.

It's a circuitous route, however, so you will need to be a little patient and able to enjoy what you find along the way. Otherwise, if the freeways are reasonably clear, and you are short on time, go for it. Here are the easiest freeway routes.

Northbound	Southbound
From Long Beach take I-710 north. Join I-405 west- and northbound, transitioning to I-10 westbound. Continue through the tunnel toward Malibu on PCH.	Follow the coast from Malibu, through the tunnel, and onto I-10. Follow I-405 south and transition to I-710. Continue south and exit at Ocean Blvd. to rejoin CA 1 eastbound.

The more restful and scenic route follows the Palos Verdes Peninsula.

SAN PEDRO–PALOS VERDES

It was once said that if all the sailor's bars and bawdy houses were closed, **San Pedro** would disappear. For this coastal city was once the roughest in the area, with its own Barbary Coast.

One bar, notorious throughout the world, was Shanghai Red's. Not only could you order anything you had the money to pay for, there was some small chance you might survive long enough to enjoy it.

In fact, the place was so tough that no regular bouncer could measure up, and for years the bar employed Cairo Mary—a woman of no small stature, with tattooed arms like oak barrels. Her specialty was a two-handed boost out into the street and straight into a lamppost. Not even the toughest sailors messed with Cairo Mary.

That's changed now. Oh, the merchant marine is still a presence here, but fading in its influence. The city has welcomed new residential development and, at middle age, is slipping into the landscaped lifestyle.

Part of the change came with development of Ports O' Call Village, one of the very first, and still among the best, of all the nouveau seaport villages. Ports O' Call is always worth a browse, a bit of lunch, plus a purchase you'd never make anywhere else, but suddenly can't live without. It's what helps fill every attic trunk.

San Pedro also has a marvelous shoreline drive, and that's where we're headed. If it's time for a bite to eat, Angels Gate Park and Point Fermin make splendid picnic areas.

Northbound	Southbound
From Long Beach, continue west on Ocean Blvd., crossing Terminal Island and the Vincent Thomas Bridge (CA 47). Exit for southbound Harbor Blvd. and continue three miles to 22nd Street. Turn right and make a left on Gaffey Street. Continue south to land's end.	From Pt. Fermin, continue north on Gaffey Street to 22nd Street. Turn right and then left on Harbor Blvd. Continue north to CA 47 and take the Vincent Thomas Bridge eastbound, crossing Terminal Island on Ocean Blvd. Continue to Long Beach.

Once part of a vast rancho, **Palos Verdes Peninsula** is still one of the most beautiful places in the entire Los Angeles basin.

Lush and rolling, Palos Verdes (green hills) remains true to the more relaxed lifestyle of California a few decades ago. Jutting into the sea as it does, the peninsula is first in line for ocean breezes. And on a good day, you can clearly see Santa Catalina Island, about twenty-two miles—not twenty-six, as in the song—away.

Three coves dot the shoreline, and even though they can be deadly in a heavy sea or tide, the coves were popular with rumrunners during Prohibition.

One of these coves, just beyond Portuguese Bend, is quite lovely. And on the north side of the highway, you'll find Wayfarer's Chapel designed by Lloyd Wright. Whatever your faith or philosophy, a few minutes in this unique place can be calming if not inspirational.

Northbound	Southbound
From Pt. Fermin, drive west along Paseo del Mar to Western Ave. Turn right, then left again on 25th St. Continue west, joining Palos Verdes Drive South. At Point Vicente, Palos Verdes Drive South will become Palos Verdes Drive West. (Don't ask.)	From Palos Verdes Blvd., join Palos Verdes Drive West and continue south. At Point Vicente, Palos Verdes Drive West becomes Palos Verdes Drive South. Exit at 25th St., turn right on Western Ave. and left on Paseo del Mar to Pt. Fermin.

There is a bit of culture shock on leaving the peninsula, with the tempo quickening along beaches to the north— where locals work at appearing laid-back while going flat out in all directions.

REDONDO BEACH–MALIBU

Although these beach cities once had individual identities—and surfers can still be pretty territorial—they have largely grown together along the highway. Only a few highlights in their history and character separate them today.

Northbound	Southbound
From Palos Verdes Drive West, transition to Palos Verdes Blvd. and then to PCH (CA 1). Continue to Herondo and turn left toward the beach. Turn right at Hermosa Ave. and continue, jogging east as it becomes Manhattan Ave., and again as the street becomes Highland Ave. Continue on as it becomes Vista del Mar, past LAX, and angle right onto Culver Blvd. Turn left on PCH and continue to Washington Blvd. Turn left to get back to the beach and right again on Pacific Ave. Continue on as Pacific becomes Neilson Way and then Ocean Ave. At California St. turn left down the incline and angle right onto PCH. Continue on until nearing Oxnard.	As PCH nears Santa Monica stay to the right. Approaching the tunnel, exit for Main St. and turn right onto Ocean Ave./Neilson Way. Continue as Neilson becomes Pacific Ave. Turn left at Washington Blvd. and angle right on Admiralty Way. Turn left at the last opportunity and right again onto PCH (CA 1). Turn right on Culver Blvd. and angle left onto Vista del Mar. Continue on as the street becomes Highland. At Manhattan Ave. jog right and then left again. Jog right at Gould as Manhattan Ave. becomes Hermosa Ave. Turn left on Herondo and right again on PCH. Continue on to connect with Palos Verdes Blvd. and Palos Verdes Drive West.

Southernmost in the span of beaches arcing up to Malibu, **Redondo Beach** suffers less from crowding. In fact, there is a fine entry to a favorite local beach at Malaga Cove. Mid-week or early in the morning, take Via Rosa or Paseo de Playa, north of the kink of Palos Verdes Drive.

This entire shoreline, from Long Beach to Santa Monica Bay, was explored by Juan Cabrillo in 1542. And even he could see that it would be a tough commute. Redondo Beach and other westside beach cities first opened up as resort areas when the Big Red Cars of Pacific Electric began making weekend runs. Still, this very pleasant vest-pocket community was too great a distance for the 9 to 5 folks. Enter the aerospace industry, with massive employers like TRW, and Redondo Beach filled up overnight. Still, the area remains somewhat secluded, near the end of the line at Palos Verdes. And with superb weather and a city-long state beach, who's complaining?

Hermosa Beach residents certainly don't complain—they're too busy. For Hermosa is the center of the good-beach-hard-body lifestyle. Everyone here is twenty-eight or possibly twenty-nine, even the mayor is a surfer, and residents spend their non-sunny hours at the gym working out. The rest of the time they make money. Crime here is virtually nonexistent—who has time to get into trouble? And they pretty much want to keep it that way. If both physical and social immortality are ever discovered, the genes will undoubtedly come from Hermosa Beach.

But for all its physical and fiscal fitness, Hermosa has strong roots in the L.A. scene of the 1940s and '50s. Hermosa was then the hippest place to be—and Howard Rumsey's Lighthouse was the innest place to go. Rumsey had been a bass player with Stan Kenton and other leading-edge bands. His pals were Chet Baker, Shorty Rogers, Shelly Manne, and all the rest—who had no real place to jam. Rumsey organized the Lighthouse All-Stars; the rest is jazz history.

The Lighthouse, at 30 Pier Avenue, still packs in the locals for a few rounds, and is one of L.A.'s longest-running beach clubs. If you're a jazz type, you may have to wade through bands like Urban Dread and Soul Finger, but the talent is here as it always was. It's a great show onstage and off.

Farther along the coast, the good surfing and good bay-watching continue, but at a more refined pace. **Manhattan Beach** and **Playa del Rey** are more bedroom communities than beach spots. These are places where Hermosa Beachers go to buy condos after they age some, get married, or find a steady teaching job.

There is no good way to get past Los Angeles International Airport. On the inland side the traffic is impossible; on the beach side it's noisy under jets taking off. But all things considered, it's better to roll the windows up for a few minutes and stay with the coast. The scenery is better and most of the time it's less congested than PCH.

As you follow Culver Boulevard, you'll notice Hughes Aircraft to the south—along with what was once the world's longest runway, and still is the longest private runway. Howard Hughes wanted plenty of wiggle room if things went sour with a test flight, which he often flew himself. But why *that* long? Was it just an ego thing? That grew more common with Hughes as his power and personal complexity grew.

Contemporaries of Hughes have a different take. The fact is, they point out from documented experience, Howard was a terrible pilot. A record-setter, yes. But sloppy in technique and insensitive. He'd already crashed his own FX-11, ruining the plane's chances and almost ending his own life.

But in the mid-1940s when the sparkling new Lockheed Constellation was just coming off the line and Hughes was the largest shareholder in TWA, he insisted on making test flights. These turned out so badly that test crews earned a hefty bonus for going up with him—and the best pilots wouldn't fly with him no matter what.

If in your secret heart you know that you're pretty ham-handed, a long runway offers both time and solace.

Venice is an odd little boom-and-bust corner of Los Angeles once known as the "Coney Island of the Pacific." But even that grand term gives no clue about the true character of the place, which remains a haven for free-thinkers and entrepreneurs.

Officially termed the Venice of America, this area was a grand dream of developers that surprisingly came to pass. An early resort found success here late in the nineteenth century and encouraged owners to plan and build an extensive series of interconnected canals, based on the Italian prototype. There would even be a St. Mark's Square built on a smaller scale, including a hotel by the same name—which still exists just off Pacific Avenue, at the end of colonnaded Windward Avenue—minus its upper floors, which were condemned in a 1962 scrap with L.A. officials.

Equipped with but one steam shovel, the bridges and concrete-sided canals were largely laid up by hand, using a small army of men using shovels and their two hands.

The result was a major miracle. For years the Venice area of Los Angeles was pretty spiffy. But the newness wore off, the gondola rides became old hat, and the canals required more and more maintenance.

With the collapse of the American economy in the 1930s, it was all over. Prices dropped, properties were vacated, and banks holding largely worthless deeds had themselves gone under.

Enter a creature known as the California Artist, who in the 1940s recognized a good deal when he saw one. Already priced out of the Laguna Beach market, these artists picked up Venice properties on the cheap. Soon, the place was a haven, not only for non-conformists and assorted poets, but all sorts of downbeat and beat-down artists.

Beats, they called themselves, or at least Jack Kerouac called them that—and in an area bounded by the Gas House, assorted all-night coffeehouses, and Gold's Gym, they moved into every unused space. For the city of Los Angeles, an intolerable situation grew worse, and if it had not been for an alliance of architects and small developers, the city would have steamrolled the whole works.

As it was, everyone began coming to their senses in the late 1960s and Venice today is again a haven for artists and free-thinkers—however upscale they have become. Many of the old structures remain, however, and as you drive through, it is not hard to see five or six decades of survival and change imprinted on each.

Along the beachfront of this entire area runs the famous oceanfront walk, a concrete thoroughfare reserved for walkers and in-line skaters, that runs for miles, from Venice and its redoubtable Muscle Beach, all the way past Santa Monica to the edge of Malibu in the north.

The walkway, once in grave danger, has recently been renovated, along with Palisades Park, and is now as beautiful as it is lively. Countless movies, and several current television series, are filmed along this stretch. In fact, the walkway and its funky oceanfront businesses are so attractive to directors, it's hard to find a day when something *isn't* being shot here.

The relatively small community of **Santa Monica** is one of the nicest sections in the L.A. area, and it has a quite different character from the beach cities to the south. In most coastal enclaves, the primary relationship for most residents—and this is no complaint, mind you—is with the beach.

In Santa Monica, residents' primary relationship is with one another. There is a tangible sense of community here. Perhaps because, with the exception of a few homes right on the sand, PCH and the palisades separate Santa Monica from the shore.

Yet all has not been peaceful here. For as with any large family, residents are of widely differing opinions. And the subject on which the community is most deeply divided is rent control.

So far it's been a see-saw battle, with rent control for tenants in for a time, but not by much. It's a classic case of democracy and capitalism in collision—tenants have the votes, landlords have the clout.

Who gets elected on any given day is anyone's guess. And the final outcome, if there ever is one, will be measured not in number of elections but across generations, so deeply entrenched are both sides. If you want an image of this interaction, imagine what it would be like if the Capulets had been tenants of the Montagues. Everything else would become a non-issue. Romeo and Juliet could have split the scene and no one would have noticed.

If the citizens of Santa Monica are divided on the issue of rent control, they continue to be firmly behind restoration and development of the city's prime attraction, Santa Monica Pier.

Built originally as little more than a sewage outfall and steamer landing, the pier has survived no-account developers, incompetent city officials (by the drove), and the worst of the Pacific storms that plague piers all along the Southern and Central California coast.

The Loof Pier, constructed in 1917, was really the first of the overwater amusement parks located here and was built by the family that had put up Coney Island's first carousel in 1876—we'll meet young Arthur Loof again in Santa Cruz. Today, their influence is still present in the dome-and-spire carousel building that greets visitors to the pier nearly eighty-five years later.

You'll recognize both the exterior and interior of the carousel building as a prime location for *The Sting,* George Roy Hill's 1973 classic, starring Paul Newman and Robert Redford. What you won't see, of course, are old-timers like the La Monica Ballroom. Even more famous in its day than the Aragon Ballroom at Venice's Ocean Park—where Lawrence Welk introduced his champagne music and bubble machine to America—the La Monica was home turf to Spade Cooley and his band.

Today, La Monica has been replaced by a new club/restaurant, named for the grand Queen Anne Revival hotel that once perched on a bluff above the pier. Arcadia, the pier's latest attraction, features Wednesday night comedy jams, gospel/jazz artists for Sunday brunch, and a host of performers all week. Superb dining as well.

The pier makes a great outing—though the rides are tubular and modern—and there are several other good restaurants, including Rusty's, a hangout for Route 66 fans from around the world.

For the L.A. area, Santa Monica is the epicenter of self-confidence. Yet it has not always been that way. Paranoia sometimes ruled here, as in many coastal communities.

In the early days of World War II, a machine-gun emplacement was situated in the center of Ocean Park Boulevard, presumably to withstand an assault on the Douglas Aircraft factory, about the only thing even remotely strategic in this community.

And in the 1950s—which were the province of Senator Joe McCarthy and not the Fonz of *Happy Days*—prefabricated bomb shelters were once the hottest sellers on used-car lots all along Wilshire Boulevard. One lot proclaimed their model to be "The Cadillac of Shelters," and in truly oxymoronic phrasing, another lot warned everyone to "Buy Now—There Is No Future."

Stretching out along the coast from the Santa Monica Pier, PCH makes its way through expensive beach homes that sit cheek-by-jowl with mangy properties and broken-down clubs, while local agencies argue among themselves. The highway also rises and falls unpredictably in landslide areas where the unstable soil is actually sliding in under the roadbed, raising it to the level of an amusement-park ride.

North of the Sunset Boulevard intersection, keep watch for a pedestrian overcrossing above the highway and the building next to it. Even though it has fallen on hard times, the building, with its beautiful Moorish architecture with tiled archways and grand entrance, is worthy of preservation. But there is a dark side here as well, for this was once Joyas, a club and restaurant owned by Thelma Todd, famous in the 1930s for her comedic talent as well as her beauty that earned her the nickname the "Ice Cream Blond." Yet for all that, Thelma Todd was found one morning in her car, dead.

The police, not wanting to offend the mob (in case they'd snuffed her) ignored the ligature marks on her neck and put her death down to carbon monoxide poisoning. Later, despite witnesses who had seen her well after the reported time of death, the case was quietly dropped and remains unsolved to this day.

As the beach side of the highway begins to open up a bit, you can see how the waves here attracted early surfers. In fact, much of the design of the surfboard as it appears today, fiberglass and resin (except with a balsa core), was developed here and dubbed the Malibu Board.

Farther on toward Point Dume, **Malibu** emerges from its strip-mall look, following the curves of hills and beaches that characterize the area far better.

Yet there is a mystery here, too. For Californians are often surprised to realize that there is no coastal railway here. After running right along the beach north from San Diego, the Southern Pacific Railway unexpectedly turns inland at Capistrano Beach, cutting diagonally across L.A.

It certainly would have made better sense to build along this once-empty coast than to lay track across populated areas of Los Angeles, blast a tunnel through the Santa Susanna Pass, and finally make it back to the shoreline at Ventura.

The answer lies with one strong-willed woman who stood off the railway and virtually everyone else for decades.

After Malibu was first visited by explorer Juan Cabrillo, the area was pretty well left to the Chumash Indians for the next quarter century. But the pueblos at Santa Barbara and Los Angeles were both developing as beef markets, so grazing rights were allowed and a land grant from the king of Spain followed for Rancho Topanga Sostomo Simi Sequit, a spread of 13,000 acres, on twenty-two miles of coastline.

Imagine the value of that property today when beachfront assessments can exceed a million dollars per front *foot*.

The rancho stayed with the original family until later claims were disallowed in 1851. The ranch was finally sold on a quit claim for $1,400 and later resold to Frederick Rindge for $300,000.

But the Southern Pacific Railway, accustomed to getting what it wanted, attempted to force a rail line from Santa Monica northward along the coast. Mrs. Rindge, a widow by then, blocked the move by constructing her own Malibu railroad—with different gauge track. Even if the SP gained control of the right of way, the Rindge family reasoned, the passengers would still be required to change trains.

The Rindge battlecry was: They shall not pass. And even though their private railroad had gone broke—with the rails foolishly shipped to Japan just before Pearl Harbor—the Rindges hung on, refusing to allow a road north over the property. They knew that both the federal and state governments were pals with railway tycoons like Huntington. The family decided not to let anyone through—not no way, not no how.

From then on the federal and state governments took turns hauling the Rindge family into court. Legal defense bills were staggering, as they always are when small men in government are able to use the taxpayers' money for a personal vendetta.

Meantime, the Rindges put up some very serious fences and hired gangs of armed men as line riders to keep out any surveyors as well as squatters and the general public. It worked, but only for a short time.

In the end, the family's resistance came to naught as the California Supreme Court determined that the state had a right to seize property for the public good. In short, the judges were saying to the Rindges: sell us a right-of-way or we'll take it. The Rindges were forced to sell for little more than $100,000, a few cents on the dollar.

Squatters made another try at grabbing portions of the land, but as property values again skyrocketed in the 1920s, Hollywood moved in. Soon Jack Warner, Ronald Coleman, Dolores del Rio, and other movie people both tall and small, had firmly established what is known today as The Colony.

So as you drive the Malibu coast, marveling as we all do at the magnificent sweep of sea and shoreline, give some thought to the Rindge family. They lost virtually everything, but it was a hell of a fight and we—along with countless surfers—are the beneficiaries. Most of the highway, from Point Dume north, is thinly populated.

Not that there aren't other reasons. For one, Malibu ranks near the top of any potential list of natural disasters: fires, floods, landslides, earthquakes, and the perennial threat of tsunamis (ocean waves triggered by a distant quake that can travel at speeds of five hundred miles an hour or more) to flatten anyone or anything located on the coast. There may even be some surfer-dudes who have erotic dreams about tsunamis. Such is the pull of the ocean on some.

Even after a recent firestorm that laid waste to a large number of Malibu homes, virtually no one is willing to move from harm's way. It's just too beautiful, with friendly, round-shouldered foothills guarding Zuma Beach, Trancas Beach, Cabrillo Beach, and more.

Beyond Zuma Beach are some of the most gorgeous vest-pocket beaches to be found anywhere. And you may want to know this: all California state parks and beaches are free—it's the parking that costs. So the trick is to find beaches where you can park free right along the highway. So keep an eye out for signs announcing state beaches and coastal access, then pull over at a convenient place and enjoy!

At about the Ventura County line, however, the landforms change abruptly. Here, the Santa Monica Mountains begin crowding their way right to the sea's edge, forcing the highway to cling to narrower stretches—and making this one of the most spectacular drives in Southern California.

Approaching Point Mugu, you'll see where a very difficult cut had to be made, leaving Mugu Rock even more isolated and forbidding. The old highway segment that winds out around the rock—and through dozens of television commercials—is literally falling into the ocean. All of which makes for a good photo stop and an interesting opportunity to walk a remnant of old US 101.

At low tide, two lifelike rocks can be seen below the section of old highway. The Chumash Indians—who once populated much of the California coast and the islands offshore—believe these rocks are the forms of Princess Hueneme (pronounced *why-nee-mee*) and her husband, a couple driven mad by a jealous witch-woman of the tribe. In her unbearable sadness, the kind and beautiful Hueneme walked out to her death in the pounding surf here. Her woeful husband followed, and for generations the Chumash left offerings to Hueneme's spirit near the base of Mugu Rock.

So when coast highway surveyors appeared after the Rindge affair, they were warned that a road here would desecrate a sacred place and thereafter begin falling into the sea. The highway did just that, requiring constant maintenance to keep the coastal link open, until it was moved back from the ocean's edge—and the two rocks.

CENTRAL COAST

OXNARD–MUSSEL SHOALS

Beyond Mugu Rock, at a pause in the rugged coastal mountains, the Oxnard Plain stretches inland for miles, offering what seems like Strawberry Fields Forever. And indeed, the area is one of the great strawberry producers, with close to year-round production.

When the fields are planted and sheathed in protective vinyl, the otherwise featureless land here takes on the look of a vast ice-rink. And for the landowner and tenant, strawberry time can be much like skating on thin ice.

A strawberry crop costs between $25,000 and $35,000 per plot to nurture and harvest. And almost anything can happen. Pacific storms, heavy Santa Ana winds, an aggressive pest, drought conditions that drive up water costs—or any combination thereof—can decimate a crop and flatten the farmers, along with the local economy.

Still, if a grower's luck holds, the harvest is truly sweet. That's because, next to marijuana, strawberries are the most profitable crop ever to come from the ground. In a good year, the dollar-yield per farm can be extraordinary.

A fine scenic drive bypasses the truck-congested downtown area of **Oxnard** and can even take less time.

Northbound	Southbound
Beyond Point Mugu NAS, exit US 101 at Hueneme Rd. and drive west toward the coast. Turn right at Ventura Rd. and then left at Channel Islands Blvd. Continue over the bridge and bend right as the street becomes Harbor Blvd. Continue about 9 miles and turn right on California St. At Main St., turn left, passing the San Buenaventura Mission (3 blocks) to rejoin US 101.	Take the Ventura Ave. exit. After a couple of blocks, turn right on Main St., continuing east past the 3-block San Buenaventura Mission. At California St., turn right again and continue to Harbor Blvd. Turn left and continue south along the coast for about 9 miles. Bend left and cross over the bridge as Harbor becomes Channel Islands Blvd. Turn right on Ventura Rd. and left at Hueneme Rd. and rejoin US 101.

Along this drive you'll be passing fields that are among the most abundant in the world—even with most of the land in untillable mountains, high deserts, and river washes, Ventura County produces and produces: $180 million annually in lemons alone, with almost that much yielded by strawberries on less than one-fifth the acreage. Toss in nursery stock and celery at about $20 million each, plus an astonishing range of vegetables, nuts, and fruits, and the total rises to $1 billion or more from not much more than 100,000 acres. Around here poor weather predictions are almost a capital offense.

If it's mealtime or you are spending the night in the
Oxnard-Ventura area—and you love really good pizza—
there's a place called Dominick's at 477 N. Oxnard
Boulevard (park in back) where they serve up a thin crust
so good it makes New Yorkers homesick. This restaurant
is also housed in an old Kaiser-Fraser dealership. And
therein lies a tale.

State historians are mad for families like the Hunting-
tons. But little is said of Henry J. Kaiser, the last great
American industrialist. He was one of the partners who
built Boulder (renamed Hoover) Dam, and a master orga-
nizer with steel and cement plants—plus the Kaiser Health
Plan—all to his credit. His impact on everyday life in California from the 1930s to the 1960s was simply enormous.

After Pearl Harbor, the U.S. discovered that it had only
about 5 percent of the merchant fleet it needed to fight a
two-ocean war—and worse news—vessels took two to
three years to complete, rivet by rivet.

Kaiser had a better idea: he had ship plans laid out life-
size, hired scads of welders and semi-skilled laborers, and
instead of riveting thousands of plates, he had substruc-
tures separately assembled, then welded together. Every
few weeks, a new Liberty Ship. Adapted from a late-
1800s design, the Liberties were slow, taking longer to
sail to Europe at ten knots than it took to build them.
(You'll have the chance to inspect one of those ships in
San Francisco.) But we needed raw tonnage, not sophisti-
cation, and Henry Kaiser gave it to us.

The new process took about thirty days—and in one
rush to glory, a shipyard actually completed a Liberty in
five days. In the end, we might have held our own in
World War II without Henry Kaiser, but we never could
have won it.

After the war, Kaiser decided to build cars, and if you
look in automotive histories, you'll see how much better
they look today than they did then. But in a market very
few understand, Kaiser-Fraser went broke.

Here in Dominick's you can see exactly what the old
dealership was like. There's the customer entrance, a
showroom at the front, with a little round-holed cashier's
window just behind, and the big overhead door at the

back. True to Kaiser's personal values, more space was given over to service than to sales.

Imagine, as you munch some of the best pizza to be found anywhere on the West Coast, how exciting it must have been to open this little dealership right after the war, with a new line of cars never seen before. Heady days, indeed.

If you are planning on spending a day in Santa Barbara, give some thought to staying overnight in the Oxnard-Ventura area and driving to Santa Barbara in the morning. It's only about forty minutes up the coast from here, but the prices for good accommodations rise sharply as you drive north.

One place to consider in **Ventura** is the venerable Pierpont Inn—a few blocks after Seaward Avenue, turn right on Sanjon (*Sanhone*) Road and right again to the Pierpont's main lobby and award-winning restaurant.

The inn opened in 1910 and in the intervening years has nearly been ruined by a series of alterations. Now, back in family hands, the Pierpont is being thoroughly restored and upgraded, as befits its marvelous Craftsman style. Most of the work should be completed by now.

Rooms are in the $100 range and up, including full guest privileges at the adjoining Racquet Club and spa. Tours of the Inn are also available. (805-643-6144)

From Harbor Blvd., a few blocks north of Seaward Ave. and south of California St., turn east on Sanjon Rd. and right at the next opportunity to the Pierpont Inn lobby and restaurant.

In Ventura, as you turn onto Main from California Street, you'll notice a striking building on the corner to your left. It's the Earle Stanley Gardner Building, named for and once owned by the mystery writer famous for his Perry Mason series. Gardner's own law practice was here, and on the completion of each new manuscript, the author-attorney went straight down to the Pierpont Inn for a celebration.

San Buenaventura Mission is one of the most overlooked of all California missions and that's too bad, for it has a retiring, provincial quality all its own—not unlike the town in which it resides. It was the ninth mission, founded by Father Serra on Easter Sunday in 1782, and his last.

Although Main Street in Ventura gives way to a murky array of thrift shops farther east, the mission district continues to be open and attractive with good adaptive reuse of existing structures.

Farther east, at 896 Main Street, is one of PCH's best hideaways. The Victorian Rose Bed and Breakfast is in a former Southern Methodist Episcopal church that has been reincarnated through the amazing grace and total commitment of its owners.

With ornately carved ceiling beams that soar thirty feet, gorgeous stained glass on every side, and its original ninety-six-foot steeple intact, the overall design blends Gothic, Norwegian, and Mission styles to produce an experience that is both exciting and tranquil.

Be prepared, however. Stepping in from the street is like walking through Alice's looking glass. Except that everything is exactly as it seems, and more. Each of the guest rooms—boasting air conditioning (a rarity here) and a gas-log fireplace—is a feast for the senses. Few guests even turn on the television sets provided, the rooms are such a treat for the eyes.

In a part of California where the sublime is often sought but seldom realized, there is nothing to compare to the one-hundred-eleven-year-old Victorian Rose or the owners' attention to their guests. If you don't have a honeymoon, a big night, or anniversary coming up, create one. This place conjures the essence of mystery and romance plus a truly marvelous breakfast, all at moderate rates. (805-641-1888)

From Ventura, you'll join the rushing 101 freeway for only a few miles, then it's possible to exit for a leisurely drive along the waterfront. This section of highway has often been washed out during severe storms (don't ask why beach homes are still built here). Hence, the freeway above is now cut well back into the mountain—where it falls prey to rockslides.

During summer months the beach area is crowded with kids, pets, and blind-sided motorhomes, so be cautious. This section is best enjoyed at slower speeds before it's necessary to rejoin the freeway.

Northbound	Southbound
Exit US 101 freeway at State Beaches and continue along the waterfront. Rejoin the freeway as necessary and exit from a left-hand turn lane at Mussel Shoals. Take care as you do, drivers often do not realize that a left-turn chute is coming up and tend to tailgate along here.	Exit to the right at Mussel Shoals and turn left into the inn's parking lot. Departing the inn, continue south and exit for an oceanfront stretch of the old highway. Rejoin the freeway at Emma Wood State Beach, over a great curving bridge still surviving from the old two-lane days.

Cliff House Inn at **Mussel Shoals** is one of those special places that could once be found in isolated splendor all along California's coast. Now, with the combined pressures of development and reservation of large areas for public use, these small hideaways are disappearing.

Somehow, Cliff House hangs on, and if it is near mealtime, or you can imagine it is, then do stop in for an intimate meeting with the past at Shoals Restaurant—a most special place to dine along the coast.

Breakfast, Sunday brunch, and lunch are best on the tiny patio where you'll be about as close to the Pacific as you can get without a soaking.

The menu is excellent as well, and the service is retro-friendly. At the shaded patio tables grouped around a small pool, all traffic noise recedes and in moments the setting will capture your heart.

Before leaving, take time to walk out on the point of rocks just above the sea to the south. Breathe in the musky sea air, look back along the shoreline, and for a moment you'll know how it all once was. And that with care some things needn't be lost. Keep that thought.

Carpinteria is more like a neighborhood than a beach town and has no plans to dress itself up as quaint. Most of the streets have no sidewalks, and where a footbridge will do instead of a major thoroughfare, that's what Carpinteria has. Santa Barbara commuters who live here find Carpinteria limiting and cultureless. The town finds them ungrateful, because by any measure, this is a pretty nice place to be.

Carpinteria once advertised its beach as the world's safest, then thought better of the potential for liability and recanted. Still, the beach here is superb and if you're looking for a town where you can wander around bare-footed, kicking up dust with your toes, this is the place.

Too often lumped together with Santa Barbara, **Montecito** has its own distinct charm. It's simply that most of it is as invisible as the spread of magnificent homes that populate this softly wooded place.

Montecito is also laid-back and quite artsy in a way that its larger, more crowded neighbor envies. Santa Barbarans meeting one another for coffee or a glass of wine often drive the few minutes south to Montecito to enjoy one of the sidewalk bistros along Coast Village Road. It's a short and pleasant drive. Take the time if you can.

Northbound	Southbound
For Montecito, exit at Olive Mill Rd. and continue straight ahead from the stop sign. Rejoin US 101 northbound at Hot Springs Rd.	Exit at Hot Springs Rd. and continue as it becomes Coast Village Rd. Cross over the freeway and rejoin US 101 from Olive Mill Rd.

There are two ways to live freely and happily in **Santa Barbara.** Be oil-stock rich or student-poor. In between it is a daily struggle to remain in what is arguably one of the most beautiful cities in the world.

Wages in the service industry are bargain-basement low, and a constant influx of graduates from the University of California—who are as determined as everyone else not to leave—creates a devastating labor market. Yet the city is so gracious and womblike in its comforts that almost any aggravation seems acceptable.

So if you find some degree of condescension among the 90 percent who work for the other 10 percent of the population here, don't take it personally. It's only that, as an outsider, you offer no advantage within the ruling socioeconomic structure. But then, neither are you a threat, which accounts for the laboratory gaze presented by so many Santa Barbarans.

That said, you may as well give yourself over to the city as most visitors do, and reap the rewards. Because Santa Barbara *is* wonderful. And like Laguna Beach, it is less a place to do, than a place to *be*. So take it in like California's winter sun.

As a practical matter, it's best to head for the Tourist

Information Center—where they have about nine million brochures—at 1 Garden Street and Cabrillo Boulevard. There are a few moderately priced lodgings and restaurants in town, and the tourism folks can save you time and frustration in finding accommodations, restaurants, and attractions of interest to you.

Whether you plan on stopping in Santa Barbara or not, there are two special drives through the city proper, other than US 101—which everyone on or off the freeway roundly hates—and which stops dead in its tracks at the least opportunity.

Both routes are scenic but in an entirely different way. The beach route is just that, while the hillside route on Alameda Padre Serra snakes along high above the city and deposits you right in front of Mission Santa Barbara. Not an easy decision.

Northbound—Hillside	Southbound—Beach
Exit at Salinas St. and continue on through the roundabout. You'll soon see that you are on Alameda Padre Serra, and climbing. Be alert to divisions in the street that put you on the high road, as the red-tiled city spreads out on your left. Continue on past Lasuen Rd., and the former campus of UCSB on your right. At the bottom of the hill, turn left at the stop for Mission Santa Barbara. From there turn left on Laguna St. and right again on Mission St. At State St. you may return to points of interest downtown by turning left, or continue on Mission to rejoin a more accommodating portion of US 101.	Exit at La Palmas and turn right, continuing past the country club and the heart of the Hope Ranch district. Bend left on Roble Dr., then wiggle-woggle until the street makes up its mind for a while, and becomes Marina Dr. Another right-left jog and you'll be on Cliff Dr. CA 225, climbing on up to what's called The Mesa. Continue to Meigs Rd. and turn right on what will be Shoreline Dr. Pass Santa Barbara City College on your left, go straight ahead at Castillo St. and you'll be on Cabrillo Blvd. At State St. you can turn left for points of interest downtown or continue past the bird refuge to rejoin US 101.

The city is dealing with the parking problem caused by attracting too many people while enforcing a no-expansion policy. The best solution is to park in a conveniently located public lot and walk. Most of what you will want to see and photograph is located in a nine-block area downtown, so it's easy to get around.

Strolling State Street is a grand pastime anyway, with coffee and juice bars from which you can comfortably ogle everyone else—and trust me, it's *great* ogling, made better by the fact that locals are not putting on a show; it's how they really are. Then, of course, there are the other oglers . . .

For still photographers especially, the Santa Barbara Courthouse and the Presidio are on the must-do list. If there is a single defining structure in Southern California today that represents the Spanish era brought right into the present it is the courthouse. It is best shot early in the day, however, or in late afternoon when the light is best and the home-video squads are less abundant. The same things can also be said for Mission Santa Barbara. Is it the most beautiful of all the missions? No. Is it stunning in its presence? Absolutely.

A couple of blocks up State Street, north of Victoria, is the Arlington, and it is hard not to go overboard for the beauty and intrigue of this courtyard theater. Perhaps even more than the courthouse and Presidio, the Arlington Theater speaks to the image and spirit of Santa Barbara—as is apparent once you experience the interior.

In Hollywood's golden era, there were many more convenient and expansive theaters in which to hold a sneak preview—and the Arlington was known for having tough audiences. Still many producers returned to the Arlington simply because it was so enchanting; one of the few times when Hollywood's heart overshadowed its wallet. Some theater buffs report that, once they were seated, and began to look around at the pueblo-style walls and blue, twinkling-star ceiling, they completely lost touch with the movie that was playing. That's probably a little over the top, but not by much. Not in Santa Barbara.

GOLETA–LOMPOC

Even as late as the mid-1950s, you could eat lunch in the middle of Hollister Avenue and likely be undisturbed. The old Marine Corps Air Station (whose original runways now serve Santa Barbara's airport) had been closed and there was little else for **Goleta** except the surrounding lemon groves and the migrants they employed. Isla

Vista was basically a collection of seaside and off-road cottages, many of which were falling apart.

Then the University of California came to town. In the mid-1950s, UC Santa Barbara moved from its Riveria and Mesa campuses into the old Marine Corps buildings up on the bluffs overlooking the sea.

Faculty members and administrators spent the first few months looking for their desks and chairs, which had been distributed almost randomly among the old wooden military structures that made up the new campus. Now the campus is undeniably a showcase and a student's delight.

If you are an architecture buff or movie fan, the Hollister-Winchester Canyon Road exit will lead you back south to an old Richfield service station of unique design, used in the 1991 remake of *The Postman Always Rings Twice*. This same site also happens to be just a few hundred yards from a story most historians don't even know.

During the early days of World War II, when practically nothing was going right for the U.S., Santa Barbarans were close by their radios to hear one of President Roosevelt's famous fireside chats. FDR had developed his informal way of talking to the American people during the depression. Now, it had equal value. People were calmed by the president's rich voice, his measured words, as he began discussing our coastal defenses.

Yet just as the president began speaking, a giant Japanese fleet-class submarine, the I-17, rose to the surface. She'd attacked the SS *Emidio* off Cape Mendocino in December, and had been skulking around San Diego a few days earlier but could find no merchant or naval targets there, so Captain Noshino brought his sub north through the Santa Barbara Channel.

On February 23, 1942, at 7:00 P.M., the I-17 surfaced. Crew members observed bright headlights along US 101, with no dimout conditions. Standing 2,500 yards offshore, the three-hundred-foot sub opened fire with a 5.5-inch gun, putting thirteen rounds into the oil facility at Ellwood Terminal, and the Winchester Canyon area.

Though U.S. historians later maligned Japanese accuracy, the truth is that the gun crew performed well, with about half the rounds hitting the storage tanks right on the button.

If you wanted to blow the whole place up, the tanks would be prime targets. That much is undeniable fact. But the rest of the story remains muddied. The I-17's documented mission was to raise enough hell to bring U.S. warships steaming down from the north into ambush. Yet, if that were true, the boat's immediate departure (i.e., bug-out) for the Home Islands makes no sense.

Some say that the submarine commander was a former tanker captain who had regularly taken on oil at the Ellwood facility for transport to Japan. And honored though he was to be helping his nation in time of need, the commander also had friends at Ellwood. The story was that he had done his duty by shelling the terminal all right. But he saw to it that none of the rounds would explode, thereby saving the Americans he knew. With the demands of both duty and friendship satisfied, he submerged. No one seems to know for sure. But stick around, we'll meet up with the I-17 again.

As you drive north, you'll notice how quickly the signs of urban life disappear. Even the freeway lanes seem desolate here and it is easier to imagine how the entire Central California coast looked from the arrival of the Franciscans in the 1700s until well into the 1930s.

Just past Gaviota and Refugio—two of the most beautiful, and generally uncrowded, beaches in California—US 101 turns inland. When the winds are up, these few miles of road can be treacherous for smaller cars and motorcycles. RVs sway ominously and drift unpredictably, so beware. A few miles beyond a rest area and the tunnel, watch for the CA 1 exit.

Military towns usually bristle with bars and tattoo parlors and marginal housing. Lompoc bristles with flowers. Dominated by the presence of Vandenberg AFB—which in the 1950s was on the Soviet Union's "A" list for prime targets—**Lompoc** has managed to retain its identity as a small farming and business community of peaceful mien.

GUADALUPE–PISMO BEACH

The clever storymaster and producer Cecil B. DeMille is credited with having invented modern Hollywood. He not only brought the industry from two-reelers into feature films, he also clearly demonstrated how depravity and moral righteousness could be blended to produce very sexy movies.

At a time when Hollywood was under increasing attack for moral decay, DeMille produced biblical epics that reveled in turpitude and revealed far more skin than any censor would otherwise allow.

Route 66 fans also know that had it not been for snow and rain, Hollywood might well have been created in Flagstaff, Arizona. And certainly copious amounts of water played a major part in DeMille's features. So much so that when he went looking for a location in which to build the Lost City of the Pharaohs he chose a vacant Pacific Coast beach at Guadalupe.

DeMille's film was the original silent version of *The Ten Commandments,* produced for Lasky-Paramount in 1923. And it was one of the first budget-busters. Set for production at $600,000, a huge amount for its day, the upper limit was blown before DeMille even had a finished shooting script.

The director was also being hounded by moralists of every stripe. For DeMille knew that S-E-X was the short spelling of M-O-N-E-Y. He also knew better than to produce smutty films that would never play in Des Moines. So he cloaked the hot stuff he wanted in religious garb.

Now DeMille needed an out-of-the-way place that could showcase the naughty splendor of the great pharaohs, as accented by hundreds of scantily clad starlets, of course. The movie would then open with God straightening Moses out on ten crucial story points . . .

DeMille put his location scouts out, but nothing interested him, until he was persuaded to visit **Guadalupe.** There, with his back to the sea, Cecil B. DeMille looked at the blowing dunes and saw . . . Egypt.

The master director led a forced march of his entire movie company to the secretive dunes of this small seaside village. And after 1,500 laborers had finished the set in 250 tons of plaster, DeMille's vision became movie reality: a city of biblical proportions. The cameras rolled, and on the final day of shooting, DeMille simply said, "That's a wrap," and abandoned the set.

For some years, travelers came to marvel at the once-splendrous Hollywood set. But all too soon, DeMille's Lost City of the Pharaohs was itself lost beneath the blowing, shifting sands.

Today, there are only a few traces of the old set showing, but you can drive out to the location—and it's not hard to stand on the same spot of road where he stood, imagining what DeMille did. There is a movement to excavate and preserve this important bit of cinematic history, and if it looks promising, the place deserves to be a national landmark.

To visit the sun-bleached bones of *The Ten Commandments* set, take the Main St. exit from CA 1 or US 101 west all the way to Guadalupe Beach. After passing through the park gate, continue on past the sand factory and up to the top of the hill. Take care in pulling off the road—the shoulder is sandy—and look to your left. At the top of the largest dune, boards from the old set jut from the sand. At least they did a while ago.

The rest of Guadalupe remains as drowsy as it ever was. Except, of course, for an uncommon presence who inhabits the Far West Tavern—which turns out a terrific steak, by the way.

There, a peg-legged guest died when he wasn't swift enough of foot to escape a fire that engulfed the building. Now his spirit taunts guests and employees alike as thumping sounds are heard, sometimes accompanied by objects that move around without apparent cause—all in a day's experience on Pacific Coast Highway.

Both **Oceano** and **Grover Beach** were slow to develop, and enjoyed a certain polarity with Pismo Beach to the north. Pismo was successful in promoting itself, but had something of a lurid past. So Oceano and Grover City went their own way—and for a time it was the way of dreamers.

Groups in both towns had momentous plans for their beachfront. Castles would rise from the sand. No doubt DeMille's earlier vision had something to do with that.

Bank funding would be impossible, of course, and nearly all venture capital was invested in Wall Street. Any funding would have to be on a subscription basis, from residents and potential buyers.

It was the fashion, in the 1920s, for families to get away

from superheated valleys lacking any form of air conditioning. But driving times were long and the visitors rarely came from large markets like Los Angeles, which were too far away.

Still, some starts were made. Streets and lighting were even being laid out along the beachfront of Oceano—when the Great Depression arrived. Money, both real and imagined, simply disappeared. The dunes crept over much of what was left.

Farther up the coast, **Pismo Beach** had its own problems. As the 1930s ground along, some fairly sordid types were working the crowds who came to the pavilions for evenings of dancing to big-band music. Rumrunners during Prohibition had been among the first. But soon the Ladies of Whenever began showing up at the dance halls. There were police raids, which usually turned up illegal drugs even back then, but the raids were mostly ineffective. Pismo Beach was just too accessible.

Gas rationing finally helped put an end to it. And most of the rascals in town were soon drafted as World War II picked up speed. The extent of national mobilization in America is today something of a mystery—even to those who lived through it. For there was virtually no family that had not given fathers or sons to the service, and nearly everyone else, like Rosie the Riveter, worked in defense plants.

In their minds, the hookers of Pismo Beach were providing an essential wartime service. Some drifted on up to Camp San Luis Obispo, but the rest stayed on in hopes of furthering relations with soldiers in the army recreation camp that had been set in Grover City.

The camp's commanding officer and his wife saw it differently. They were determined to keep clean-cut American boys on the straight and narrow—by which they meant out of the houses in Pismo Beach. During this period, because there was no place the GIs could find breakfast, the women of Grover City joined together and cooked it for them.

After the war, with its pier and beach rentals, Pismo Beach began drawing visitors from as far away as Los Angeles. This clammer's paradise became an offbeat retreat for many of Hollywood's elite. And with the new postwar cars, it was an easy drive to the clam capital of the West.

And the Pismo clam has been the city's mainstay over the years. Once harvested at a rate of nearly 50,000 annually, the beds have become so depleted that unlimited clamming is no longer allowed. The limits were slow in coming but are sound enough to offset concerns about extinction, which would have ended the huge Clam Festival held each October.

There are a number of motor inns and restaurants, plus festivals of every sort to attract tourists. One of the biggest attractions, held during the third weekend in June, is a terrific car show with over eight hundred entries.

At mealtime, F. McClintock's Saloon & Dining House is a restaurant tradition that has made regulars of folks from as far away as Santa Barbara and Morro Bay. The place features family dining at its best, and sometimes, most boisterous.

Originally Mattie's Tavern, a converted farmhouse on US 101, the restaurant continues under caring and inventive ownership. Food and service have been ranked among the top 100 restaurants in the nation.

McClintock's is more vegetarian-tolerant than vegetarian-friendly, but you can choose a pasta dish or— more creatively—load up on their terrific appetizers. Try the Jalapeño Poppers and the Texas Toothpicks. Also, be sure not to miss the servers' skill in filling a water glass from three feet up.

McClintock's is on the inland side of US 101 at 750 Mattie Road. You can't miss it, the place is right next to city hall. It is popular so reservations are important.

Another excellent restaurant, and longtime resident, is Giuseppe's, at 891 Price Street. Like many places along the Central Coast, Giuseppe's has passed through several identities and owners, all without losing touch with its place in the community.

When built in 1920, the restaurant was called Plessas Tavern and was just about first in line for traffic coming down Price Street, then US 101. But the elite stopped in as well. William Randolph Hearst, dabbling heavily in everyone else's movie business by then, often stopped

in along with his main lady, Marion Davies, plus Carol
Lombard and Clark Gable, and a regular company of San
Simeon regulars.

Giuseppe's continues in the same tradition, with re-
gional specialties from Bari (Remember the long dialogue
in *The Bridges of Madison County* about Bari?) on the Adri-
atic. Bread here rises each day more often than Lazarus
(four times, to be exact) and the wood-fired pizzas are
splendid, as are Giuseppe's other country Italian dishes.
No reservations are accepted, but you may want to be
among the early birds.

SAN LUIS OBISPO–MORRO BAY

From coastal sand dunes and rocky bluffs with a view of
forever, the land under the coast highway changes dra-
matically as the road turns inland. Rough hills are thinly
populated with live oak and the soil itself is shaded with
mineral deposits.

On the west side of the highway at Higuera Road,
you'll see a major exposure of what might be mistaken
for copper, but it's serpentine—California's state rock.

If you are driving through in the summer, **San Luis
Obispo** may be a quick reminder of how hot the interior
valleys of California can get. Otherwise, it is a pleasant
town, blessed with a lovely mission—where it is said that
the curved, red clay tiles that mark much of California
were first produced—and one of the two Cal Poly campuses.

The Madonna Inn, still a prime destination for honey-
mooners, with its let's-pretend motifs (the Love Nest and
the Caveman Room for starters), is a dandy place to have
lunch and do a little exploring. Be sure to check out the
men's urinal disguised as a waterfall, and other restroom
surprises.

A favorite stop for breakfast-brunch-lunch-anytime
travelers between L.A. and northern cities has for years
been the homey Apple Farm at the Monterey Street
exit. Now the Farm has expanded into a major motel-
restaurant, and if the gingham atmosphere is a little extensive, the service is still warm and friendly, and the food
still vegetarian-friendly and well-prepared.

Before leaving San Luis, you might take a moment to

check out a bit of Americana. For the motel was invented right here in 1925. And the place where an entire industry—plus a new way of touring—appeared on an oak-dotted hillside is just off the present-day Monterey Street exit.

Now operating as the Motel Inn, the original motel idea was to lure motorists with a major facade out front (in this case, a mission-style belltower), then scoot everyone around back where everything was much smaller in scale.

Unlike citified hotels, which usually took your car away from you at check-in, the motel lets you park-and-pack so close to your room that you could trip over your own car bumper. The motel concept was so good, its creator even trademarked the word and put up a sign explaining to guests how to pronounce it.

Now, whether you travel a great deal or not, it would be hard to pass a single day without saying *motel* at least once.

Heading back toward the coast, the landforms change again—rolling hills and ranchland marked by knobbly outcroppings. The first will be just to the southwest as you depart San Luis. These are volcanic plugs (called *morros*), arranged in a fairly straight line all the way to the ocean. See how many you can count along the way.

East of **Morro Bay** on CA 1, you'll see glimpses of the old highway alternating to the right and left of the present alignment. Some of this original concrete dates from 1923 and suggests how narrow-framed cars had to be in order to pass one another on these narrow, twisting stretches.

Nearing Morro Bay, take the Los Osos exit, and you'll see the morros line up. How many did you count? Anything above five is an excellent score—along with Morro Rock, they're called the Seven Sisters.

Stay on South Bay Boulevard, and turn right on State Park Road, before the bridge, then bend left at the Y. Along this beautiful drive, you'll find the Natural History Museum—worth a visit, especially if you are interested in wetlands and wildlife. The rookery is a bit farther on. And keep watch for the Inn at Morro Bay, one of the very nicest (and most romantic) places along the Central

Coast. Drive in and have a look around this wayside charmer. If you aren't already married, when you see this inn, you'll want to be . . .

Continue on Main Street, and at Marina, turn left, then right on Embarcadero, and you'll be right on the waterfront of Morro Bay, on your way to the rock.

Basically, Morro Bay is a comfortable community arranged around the one inescapable feature of the entire area, which in itself is a reminder that not all California's excesses have occurred in recent years.

Tourism was just beginning to arouse interest here in the 1930s, and it was decided to construct a causeway from Morro Rock to the shore, some three hundred yards away. At the time it was believed by Realtors and business owners that far more visitors would come to see this huge volcanic plug if they could get right up close.

But where to quarry all the stone needed to construct such a heavyweight project? The answer was not long in coming. Why, from Morro Rock itself!

As the years passed, millions of tons of rock were blasted from the face of the dome. And private contractors were soon eyeing Morro Rock as a great quarry site for stone to be used in porches, garden walls, and fireplaces—talk about killing the goose that laid the golden egg.

Fortunately, the state of California stepped in, and declared Morro Rock a sanctuary to protect the endangered peregrine falcons that make the rock their home. Today you can still see the falcons as they make their two-hundred-mile-an-hour dives—and thanks to conservationists, you can still see most of Morro Rock.

On the divided highway north out of town, look to the east at the Main exit, and you'll see a marvelous Art Deco building that highlights the nature of Morro Bay.

The building was a scruffy Quonset hut. But the owner had some talented folks working for him, so they sketched out a new facade that drew its inspiration from the Coca-Cola building in Los Angeles and the owner's hometown theater. Now this portholed beauty stands there for all to enjoy.

And they do. The owner is frequently approached by someone who recalls dancing in the place or having a drink there, when in fact it has never been anything but a Quonset hut, used for storage.

CAYUCOS–CAMBRIA

The short section of freeway north from Morro Bay ends at **Cayucos** and CA 1 continues on toward Big Sur as one of the most remarkable two-lanes in the world. Largely a dirt road well into the 1930s, California's Highway 1 attracted few visitors despite its glories. Families of lighthousekeepers and a few hardy Europeans out to tour the world accounted for most of the traffic.

But by the '60s, CA 1—and Big Sur—had been truly discovered and everything from flashy sportscars to tie-dyed VW Microbuses prowled its length. At one end of the drive was the Monterey Peninsula. At the other, Cayucos.

Yet, despite its location, almost no one notices Cayucos. You'd think something major would have developed there, but no. The highway just whips right past the place.

Too bad, for Cayucos has the potential for becoming another Laguna Beach, another Sausalito. Weather is good and the town is home to a small band of artists, musicians, and antiquers—and that's how popularity often begins. A grocery store and a couple of pubs satisfy most of the town's needs, without the need for traffic signals or squads of crimefighters.

North of Cayucos, it's possible to catch glimpses of old CA 1 off to the right, winding along the bluffs and canyons, looking exactly how a road through this land should—while the newer highway blasts ahead in a straight line.

According to official sources, a town must have a post office to qualify as such—a village need only have a church. Hamlets lack both. **Harmony** has a post office, upon which the outlying ranches depend, and against which neighboring buildings lean. But if you venture in to buy some on-the-road stamps—and there could be no better place to do that—you may need to scrunch down a little, for the postmaster himself is on the tall side, and the post office was built in 1914, when people were of considerably less stature.

Although a CalTrans sign states the population of Har-

mony as eighteen, it's really a case of *more or less.* Because
only one residence in the town is occupied. The rest of
the population is scattered among ranches in the surrounding area. All this may well leave the town, like
Cayucos, poised on the cusp of greatness.

For now, it is probably the smallest of all the places
you'll encounter on Pacific Coast Highway. By comparison, Humptulips, Washington, is a metropolis at three
hundred. Harmony also has the greatest number of antique and collectibles shops per capita on the West Coast.

So take a moment to say hello. You'll be able to tell
everyone back home, in ten years or so, that you remember Harmony when it was barely more than a hamlet.

The first exit for **Cambria** will put you on old CA 1,
as it winds through the arroyos and across creeks in its un-
hurried way into town, allowing you the feeling of what it
was to travel this highway in its heyday.

Cambria itself seems to materialize from the roadside,
in part as it once was. There's a grammar school here,
looking just as it should, and farther along is the diminu-
tive Santa Rosa School, now a gallery. The town is a re-
freshing place to stroll, and picturesque without making a
struggle of it, though the Cookie Crock Market may be a
little over the top.

There are really three Cambrias: East Village, West
Village, and a section along Moonstone Beach. Toward
the western end of town, you'll find the lens from Piedras
Blancas Lighthouse—certainly worth a few minutes.

Inside a lightstation, a fresnel lens of this size and complexity is framed by the larger structure. But outside that
physical context, the lens is a clear reminder of how difficult the pouring, grinding, and safe transport of such a
slug of glass must have been.

SAN SIMEON–BIG SUR

From sheltered Cambria, it is a surprise to find the coast
even more desolate than before. This is a wild place, un-
tamed. And exactly what William Randolph Hearst, the
great manipulator, enjoyed. A place that could take the
full measure of his personal force.

Most of us have a material side and the Hearst Castle
certainly appeals to that part of our nature. It's hard to

look at giant candlesticks, crafted from silver so pure that they are literally sagging from their own weight, and not be impressed. Now maintained—that's the crucial word—by the state, the Hearst property is preserved in one of those rare arrangements where descendants of independent wealth and the people mutually benefit.

And the Hearst estate (it is much more than a "castle") is certainly an eyeful. If you feel that this may be your only trip to the Central Coast, it is well worth a visit. There are several tours, however. So a little research beforehand is a good idea.

So is perspective. Leland Stanford founded and funded what has become one of the finest universities in the world; Henry Cowell provided for both by granting both redwoods and a building site for the University of California at Santa Cruz; William Randolph Hearst, with assets of a quarter of a billion (pre-inflationary) dollars, built a monument to sheer excess. If you visit, it helps to keep that in mind.

But opposite the entrance to Hearst Castle is San Simeon State Park arcing along a cove just inside the pier, a beautiful spot to complement the huge landholdings that Hearst's father amassed. Whether you plan to visit the castle or not, take a left here for a cruise through the park, perhaps a picnic, and a look at the real San Simeon.

The town is just a dot of a place, and continues in its role of supporting player. It first served as a whaling center and Sebastian's Store (and B&B) is the only surviving structure from that period. Later, when Hearst began bringing in building materials by the kiloton and artisans by the gross, the town became a private shipping terminal with its own narrow-gauge railroad. The 1878 barn near the pier was on hand for that operation. Residences in town, done in a beautiful Mission Revival style, were built to house Hearst staff. On a clear day, it's possible to stand near old San Simeon and see the palace on the hill. It's an interesting comparison.

Beyond Piedras Blancas, the coast highway gets down to business. The bluffs become more angular, more sharply defined, as they increase in height, and push ever closer to the sea, forcing the road to respond. Here, the wind becomes almost palpable. Hawks have no need of supporting thermals here, but hang stationary in the air, flying the rising wave of sea air rushing against these bluffs.

On days when the sun seems weaker than usual, mists blow like veils into the coastal arroyos, making complete the mystery of this place. The various ways nature has of combining rock and wave are endless and justify nearly any cost of keeping this highway open.

In 1963, when one of California's not-infrequent landslides overtook a portion of CA 1, the highway was closed for a year and repairs cost almost $7.5 million to complete. Yet when the road was first constructed the entire ninety-mile project cost only $10 million. Even in depression-era dollars that's dirt cheap. The reason: prison labor.

Convicts from infamous San Quentin lived in work camps along the course of the road and toiled over the highway for nearly two decades, from 1919 to 1937. With an unending source of virtually free labor, the state was in no great hurry to complete the project. Nor were the convicts for that matter. They were beyond San Quentin's walls and earning roughly 50 cents an hour.

Better still, for every two days they labored, the convicts' sentences were reduced by three days. As earned-release programs go, this version worked pretty well.

Across from downtown **Lucia,** on a thumb-sized knob, rests one of the most delightful lunch spots you'll find along the route. Even a cup of tea here is a serene experience, for the structures and site are in such accord that it's difficult to imagine one without the other.

Father north keep watch for Nepenthe, one of the most-photographed restaurants ever, and if contemporary, Mount Rushmore architecture is your style, be sure to make a stop at Ventana. For rustic souls, Big Sur Inn is almost obligatory and moderately priced, with charming mini-lodges.

After miles of sheer-drop shoreline, with every bend in the road revealing a new, almost unbelievable view of the coast, it's easy to go into overload.

But leave room to take in Julia Pfeiffer Burns State Park or Pfeiffer Big Sur State Park. These are among the most haunting and beautiful places you'll find. A picnic here is memorable, a night spent camping here is far more.

Few experiences can top waking to dawn mists drifting silently through redwood branches a hundred feet up, or a simple breakfast accompanied by short-wave Koto music from Japan on an antique Zenith. In the soft humming of the old vacuum tubes, the past frames the moment, brings a hundred pasts to bear.

NOTE: If you are short on time through this stretch—as is commonly the case—the coastal redwood groves near Santa Cruz offer an even greater opportunity, with an interpretive walk through the great trees that is second to none, and a steam-train ride in the bargain.

On Point Sur, that past comes alive again at Point Sur Light, a reassuring beacon first lit for seamen in 1889. The station is accessible through tours available from knowledgeable docents who themselves are working on the light's difficult future.

Survival of another kind is linked to this site, though nothing remains but the history of a bygone era—a time when great silver airships flew the world's air-oceans. Nearly three hundred feet long and over one hundred feet high, the dirigibles of the 1930s could stay aloft for five days—even drifting, if need be, on the lift of almost seven million cubic feet of helium.

Powered by rows of inboard engines that rumbled along at altitude, these great airships and their sound were as familiar to residents along this coast as the UPS truck is now. Those who saw them agree that dirigibles were perhaps the most beautiful things ever designed and flown by man.

No heavier-than-air craft can compare, and the navy's USS *Macon* regularly flew this coast from her base at Moffett Field south of San Francisco.

Macon was a brilliant design, brought in at half her sister ship's cost, well-commanded, and crewed by airmen of unchallenged experience and ability. That much is known from the fact that when an unrepaired upper fin separated, Lt. Commander Herbert Wiley—despite a cascading series of failures—brought his ship gently to the sea with the loss of only two of the eighty-one men aboard.

Now she lies in 1,500 feet of water three miles south, off Point Sur. A navy research submersible found her there in 1990, blessed the remains, and left them undisturbed.

Throughout the drive, from San Simeon north, the weather orchestrates a caprice of cloud and mist. On a clear day, the mist may suddenly form, canceling out any of the view sites. Yet even on the worst fogger, a rent may appear in the cloud cover, opening up miles of sun-bright coastline. It takes some getting used to.

Finally, no commentary on Big Sur would be complete without reference to wildlife, and the herds of (Ford) Mustangs seen galloping south daily. Even when the entire coast is socked in, intrepid drivers and their long-suffering passengers brave the drifting cloud. Hatless and wind-blown, with the top down, they are valiantly getting their money's worth.

Some day, a rental agency will see the marketing possibilities here and offer corporate baseball caps free with any convertible upgrade. Meantime, if you're southbound, check the heater, just in case.

Of the many side trips off Pacific Coast Highway, a top contender is the short, twenty-mile drive inland to **Salinas** and Steinbeck Country. There are Steinbeck haunts to visit in Carmel, plus Cannery Row in Monterey. But all these can be better appreciated—and enjoyed—by first visiting Salinas and the National Steinbeck Center.

There you will find one of the finest exhibits of its kind in the world—and it's only been open a short time, so you'll be among the first to tell everyone back home about it.

Words like *multimedia* and *interactive* are darlings of the electronic age and greatly overused. Still, they apply here: clips from Hollywood films and documentaries, plus books, papers, and personal items, are brilliantly woven into a self-guided tour that invites you not only to see and hear, but to touch and smell, too.

Along the way you'll encounter the aroma of old Cannery Row, as it wafts in from a display. And standing in front of a boxcar, you'll even feel the cool draft of ice melting, in a reminder of the tragic scene from *East of Eden*. You'll also discover Rocinante from *Travels with*

Charley—yes, Steinbeck's original camper—in a place of honor.

The town of Salinas and its surroundings will bring to mind Steinbeck's stories, too, like Gabilan Street and the mountains for which it was named, that became the name given to *The Red Pony*.

If you know little of Steinbeck, his literary contributions, his lifelong struggle for migrant farmworkers, or the role he played in World War II, you'll be deeply impressed by the exhibits. And if you do a bit of writing yourself, or are simply in awe of the man's ability and the way he met life head-on, you may find partway through this tour that you've come to regard John Steinbeck as a kindred spirit—a friend and teacher.

There's a homey little café within the center, too, just perfect for lunch or a morning muffin. And the Museum Store is stocked with books and other items you'll never see on commercial shelves. The entire experience takes only a couple of hours and could well become one of the highlights of your tour. Open every day from 10 A.M. to 5 P.M., except Thanksgiving, Christmas, and New Year's Day.

The National Steinbeck Center is located at the very end of Main St. Follow CA 68, which is South Main St., on into Oldtown Salinas. In front of the building, make a careful right into the parking lot. When leaving the center, follow Salinas St. in the opposite direction, through a left bend, and turn right onto westbound CA 68, South Main St.

The easiest way to Salinas is to depart CA 1 at Monterey and follow CA 68 into the valley. The highway is vastly improved and offers easy passage through the same gap in the mountains that the fog uses.

However, if you are comfortable driving in the mountains, there is a scenic drive departing CA 1 at Carmel Valley Road (G16) and following Route G20 over Laureles Grade at 1,200 feet. This route offers both an intimacy with the land from Steinbeck's *Pastures of Heaven,* plus spectacular views of the coastline below Carmel, before connecting with CA 68 just east of Laguna Seca. Taking Laureles Grade on your way into Salinas and following CA 68 all the way when returning makes a good combination.

On your way back to the coast, you may find yourself even more curious about the fields flanking the highway—especially if it's berry season. Like the plantings in coastal Oxnard, strawberries are a prize crop here in the Salinas Valley, along with raspberries, artichokes, lettuce, and most everything you'd expect to find in your salad.

For much of the year, a billowing coastal fog sluices through a gap in the mountains to the west, flooding the valley at night and keeping temperatures down until midday. This is in no way typical of inland California valleys and is responsible for Salinas's abundance.

Along the highway you may find yourself marveling anew at fields and crops stretching to the mountains. Also keep watch for the work of artist John Cerney, whose larger-than-life figures and murals dot CA 68 and the area around Salinas.

One pair of figures, Cerney's eighteen-foot "Tribute to Farmer and Farmworker," stands on the north side of CA 68 at Spreckels Boulevard. It is a reminder that these fields are planted and harvested by a sometimes-uneasy partnership.

It is often said, in defense of a system that has been in place since the Franciscan planters of the 1700s, that the landowners are at greatest risk and therefore entitled to the larger share of the result, no matter how large that share may be.

Yet no one could be at greater risk than those who till and harvest the fields by hand. It is true that when a crop fails, the owner can be badly stung. Yet it is no less true for the worker, who may in a good year make near-poverty wages, and in a bad year make nothing at all. *Fair* has rarely applied to America's imported peasantries.

So you may be asking: why do the workers, 90 percent of Mexican heritage, stay here? Why do they labor in these fields, stooped flat at the waist for days and months at a time, in a posture that college athletes can endure for only a few hours? If it is so bad, why do they not go back across the border?

The answer is that in Mexico the workers and their families might make $5 a day if they are lucky, and doing so, will surely starve. Here, they have the faint hope of a chance—if not for themselves, then for their children, or their children's children. But even that kind of hope, as you can imagine, is an iffy business for people with a life expectancy of only fifty years.

Of course, some will argue there *has* been change. And that, too, is true. When the heartful Cesar Chavez began to organize the workers into a fair-bargaining force, conditions did improve for a time. Yet, with the death of Chavez, the flame went out.

So they labor on, silently, with some hope and little complaint—while we pass by and notice them so little that by the time tonight's dinner is over, their presence will have vanished along with our hunger.

Still, if we can realize something of this ability we have to ignore what is all around us, and we learn from that, our own journey will have mattered in a new way.

MONTEREY PENINSULA

When the sea mists blow through the trees at evening, it's hard to find a more seductive spot on the Central Coast than the Monterey Peninsula. So it's just as well that property values are sky-high and traffic conditions monumental; otherwise, we'd all live here.

Hollywood is quick to spot a good thing, of course. Over thirty-four movies have been filmed in and around the peninsula. No doubt you already knew about the brooding *Play Misty for Me* and *Cannery Row.* But did you know that *Lassie Come Home, The Graduate,* and *Star Trek IV* were filmed here as well? Rent a video tonight, visit the location tomorrow.

You could start with the Sardine Factory on Fisherman's Wharf, featured in *Play Misty for Me,* as well as picturesque sections of PCH.

Yet for all its homey look today, the village of **Carmel** was originally established as a haven for one-night stands among the Bay Area's elite. Evangelist Aimee Semple McPherson had a sweet little hideaway in town where she consorted with Radio Ray, her broadcast engineer. There's even a folk song about their affair, because such matters are never secret for very long.

One clue to the town's past is that there are still no house numbers here, just lot designations. If you want your mail, you stand in line—once the local post office is sure that you are you—and receive mail at the window along with everyone else.

E-mail, as you might guess, is very popular with Carmelites. Trees are special here, too, and each one in town is registered. Neon signs and parking meters have also received special attention in Carmel—there are none.

If all this sounds quaint to the point of being medieval, you have only to look about at the charm Carmel has managed to create and retain. It is just beautiful.

Shopping at The Barnyard, south of town at Carmel Valley Road, makes the point. It is unhurried and appealing even to men whose preferences are more in tune with Pep Boys. This small retro-mall is great for browsing and offers a perfect deli source for a picnic lunch south at Point Lobos—a major stop in an area with a must-see on every corner—or at Point Sur.

Back in town, even lunch at the Hog's Breath Inn, on San Carlos, between Fifth and Sixth, belies its name. Good food, fine service. The Inn is owned by Clint Eastwood and is in the tradition of a man who directed his first film here (*Play Misty for Me*) and returned to offer even greater service as a mayor with good judgment and a superb sense of timing for sensitive issues that come with the territory.

But many locals will argue that Clint's greatest gift to the people of Carmel was the eleventh-hour save and full restoration of Mission Ranch, now one of the finer inns on the Central Coast, and an excellent place to dine, even if you can't stay over.

Mission Ranch, especially the bar, remains planted squarely in the 1930s and '40s. And it has developed a loyal following over the years. From near-speakeasy days, through service as an officers' club during World War II, the bar has managed to retain a special sense of place reminiscent of Goulding's in Monument Valley, where director John Ford once held court.

Today, the Mission Ranch Restaurant and Bar still echo to songs from earlier days, sung by regulars—and strangers willing to join in. But it's not group karaoke. This is fellowship and camaraderie in a time when that is becoming a hard thing to find. You'll find ample drinks here, along with vegetarian-friendly lasagna and ribs so good that many locals will order nothing else.

Whether you are a fifth-degree Eastwood fan or not, Mission Ranch isn't to be missed. It is one of those rare places where a gift from the past joins with the present.

Two undervisited sites in the Monterey area include the lovely Carmel Mission Basilica, at 3083 Rio Road, near the southern end of Junipero Avenue. Few people realize that this was the second mission constructed—they were not built in geographic order—or that Father Serra, who established the entire California mission system, is interred here.

Even fewer travelers know that a rival to the beauty of Seventeen Mile Drive makes a circuit of **Pacific Grove**—and it's free. You can make it part of a grand tour by proceeding from Fisherman's Wharf along Cannery Row to Ocean View Boulevard, and rounding the tip of Monterey Peninsula.

Along the way from Fisherman's Wharf, there are a few points of special merit, first being the Monterey Bay Aquarium. The only habitat—and the largest—of its kind anywhere, Monterey's aquarium is devoted entirely to marine life of a specific region: the Central Coast of California.

It's said that the aquarium's plan was first derived from a small sea of tequila under active investigation by several marine biologists. Scientists all, they were not satisfied with the resources available to them or the public on the Central Coast. No doubt the tequila contributed to the scale of their ideas, including the million-gallon tank and 300,000 sea creatures found at the aquarium today.

Which brings Ed "Doc" Ricketts to mind, of course—central character of Steinbeck's *Cannery Row,* and the man who changed the face of marine biology in the region, and perhaps the world.

Now, it is not known what brand of tequila these amiable scientists were drinking, or whether Doc Ricketts was present in spirit (or spirits). But his pioneering efforts in the 1930s were certainly known to the aquarium's creators, and resides in their work today.

Further along your circuit of the peninsula, you'll notice Pacific Grove's own brand of charm. Back in the late

1800s, when tent revivals were in vogue, Pacific Grove became popular as a tent city for summering Methodists. They could hardly stay in Carmel, could they? But many did stay on in Pacific Grove, building the stately Victorian homes for which the city is now widely known.

Though long gauzy skirts have remained popular over the years, high-button shoes have given way to sneakers—and the Victorian homes have become a collection of shops, plus bed-and-breakfast inns (B&Bs), and excellent restaurants.

Point Piños Lighthouse is equally a part of the community, with a beacon that has shone continuously since 1855. Also watch for the Pacific Grove Museum of Natural History, where you'll find a life-sized sculpture of a California gray whale, plus exhibits and a brief video on Pacific Grove's continuing love affair with the Monarch butterfly.

Take care how you drive in Pacific Grove, however. Bumper stickers here declare: "I Brake for Butterflies," and it's a worthy practice. There is also a city ordinance, first passed in 1939, authorizing a $1,000 fine for molesting a butterfly in any way. For the gentle people of Pacific Grove care deeply for the Monarchs, give them sanctuary, and are rewarded by one of the grandest and most delicate displays nature has to offer.

Each year, during wintering season from mid-October to mid-February, millions of these orange-and-black beauties cluster in the Butterfly Trees just east of Washington Park and in the Monarch Grove Sanctuary.

Local volunteers work hard to maintain the butterflies' habitat and each year the Monarchs return. To do so, the butterflies typically fly 2,000 miles at altitudes of up to 10,000 feet—no small feat for an insect far more delicate than the smallest hummingbird. Yet below a temperature of fifty-five degrees—and when they are mating—these lovely creatures are exceptionally vulnerable. So if they are present when you visit, drive slowly and take care where you step.

Now here is the most remarkable part of the story. For the returning Monarchs are four or five generations removed from the butterflies who made their annual flight east into the valleys and mountains the prior spring. What marvelous genetic code is passed from parents to off-spring to enable such complex behavior? And what behavioral codes might we ourselves be carrying, of which we remain largely unaware?

To visit the butterfly habitats on a circuit of the peninsula, continue past Point Piños Light Station and follow Sunset east to Seventeen Mile Drive.

If you wish to see how the other half (or maybe more by now) of our own species lives, turn right and enter at the gate. Otherwise turn left and drive north less than a half-mile. Washington Park will be on your right, and a little farther on, Monarch Grove Sanctuary is on the left at Pico Avenue.

SEASIDE-APTOS

On CA 1 again, at the exit for Fisherman's Wharf, the rock-bound coastline that has become so familiar over the last hundred miles simply disappears into endless dunes. Small wonder settlers following in the Franciscan's footsteps made Monterey their final stop.

Seaside and **Marina** were both linked, one way or another, to the giant Fort Ord complex. And as military spending dropped, they suffered. But camp towns have a way of adapting, and now that California State University has taken up residence here, both towns will forge ahead.

Marina's lodgings are somewhat less costly than Monterey, if you don't mind staying farther out. But if you are doing the coast on a tight budget, check out properties in Seaside, where there is a quantum drop in pricing—to $50 or less.

You will also be reminded, as you continue driving along California's shoreline, that there is an unwritten rule somewhere that compels power companies to place gigantic, eye-stopping power plants in the most scenic of all locations.

Moss Landing is one of those places that changes little. The structures are resolute and properly weathered, and the fleet of fishing and pleasure boats is largely of wood. Here, their seams remain sound, even though they would open in the warmer waters of Southern California.

This portion of CA 1 is quite congested and it doesn't get much better for some miles, so take a few minutes to drive straight through Moss Landing where horses will watch you from the balconies of antique stores.

In the fields flanking the highway for some miles, you'll see what look like big furry pineapples. The tiniest little centers of this agricultural shrubbery turn up in the supermarket as artichokes, and **Castroville** is the production center for these tasty little marvels.

If you're a hiker, you might want to check out Nisens Marks State Park near **Aptos,** with a 10,000-acre forest and Aptos Creek Trail, epicenter of the 1989 Loma Prieta quake in Santa Cruz County.

Approaching **Capitola-by-the-Sea,** be alert for the Park Avenue exit from the highway.

The Santa Cruz area is made more beautiful by its waterways, but crossing town can be confusing unless you give yourself up to the process. And the drive is worth it.

After the freeway's crush, Park Avenue offers a tree-shaded entry to this unhurried side of Monterey Bay. Odd, too, for the gentrified Spanish influence that peaks in Monterey, all but disappears here on the north side, after its collision with Yankee culture. (In fact we'll drive by the spot where those two cultures met in uneasy partnership.)

So from this point northward, you will see virtually no tile roofs. And roadside churches—from Russian Orthodox to hip nondenominational—will bring constant surprise after such uniformity.

Northbound	Southbound
For a more relaxing drive and a scenic route into Santa Cruz, exit at Park Ave. and head southwest toward the beach. Turn left on Monterey Ave., round the Esplanade and turn left again on Portola Drive. Continue as it becomes Cliff Drive at the lagoon. Jog right five blocks on 7th Ave. and turn left again on Eaton, which later becomes Murray. (Hang on, we're almost there.) Bend right as the street becomes East Cliff Drive again. Turn left on Riverside Ave. and right onto Beach St., and you are at the boardwalk. On departure, go west on Beach St. and angle left onto West Cliff Dr., which you follow for several miles. Turn right on Swanton Blvd., left on Delaware, and right again on Natural Bridges Dr. A left on Mission St. will take you to CA 1.	For a scenic and uncongested route into Santa Cruz, exit from CA 1 at Mission St., turn right on Natural Bridges Dr. Jog left on Delaware Ave. and right on Swanton Dr. Bend left onto West Cliff Dr. and continue for several miles. At Beach St., turn right. You'll be at the spiritual center of Santa Cruz. On departure, or to continue on to Capitola, turn left on Riverside Ave. and right on East Cliff Dr. across the bridge. Bend left as the street becomes Murray and then Eaton St. Turn right on 7th Ave. and a few blocks later, left on East Cliff Dr., which reappears for a bit and then becomes Portola Dr. Bend right onto Esplanade, which swings left and becomes Monterey Ave. Just across the tracks, turn right onto Park Ave. and continue to CA 1.

The Santa Cruz experience begins with Capitola-by-the-Sea, where the laid-back California look carries an eastern undercurrent, and a reminder that railroads were once California's main thoroughfares. In fact, the spur line, which runs through here and up to Davenport, was once an important rail connection, with a stylish depot built in 1901, and the pride of Capitola.

Of course, as rail traffic declined and passenger service was eliminated, Capitola's depot soon found itself in ruin. In 1960, the structure was sold by Southern Pacific for $1, turned 90 degrees to face the street, and partially restored.

Now, under its present ownership, the Inn at Depot Hill, 250 Monterey Avenue, (still next to the old tracks) has earned a place among the finest inns on the West Coast. Designers and enchanted strangers often tour the place, relishing the fine touches and perfect vision of its innkeeper.

With twelve guest rooms and service that includes full

breakfast, a wine-and-cheeese hour, plus an evening dessert (cherry cheesecake, if you're lucky), the property easily earns its four-star rating. If space is available, and you can manage it, Inn at Depot Hill can make a stay in the Santa Cruz area an event in itself. Rooms and suites range from $195 to $275 per night and offer good value for a resort area, plus an unbeatable sense of place. (800-572-2632)

Capitola is another of those beachside resorts that began as a tent city. Today, its Mediterranean look is captivating, and it offers a quiet place to stroll among browser-friendly shops and a number of excellent restaurants and pubs. In addition, the view of Monterey Bay is such that artists are sometimes as thick as tourists here.

And Capitola sees to its own. Stuck with an old movie theater in a leftover Quonset hut, the town has transformed it into the Capitola Theater for the Performing Arts. And in its beachy Art Deco style, it works.

Next door, **Santa Cruz** is nothing less than magical. It embraces an eclectic university, a historic amusement park, magnificent redwood groves, and a south-facing beach that creates a year-round climate envied by all of Northern California. How all this came to be, in light of settlement by Yankee mountainmen and lumberers of the roughest sort, is nothing short of amazing.

Yet Santa Cruz, for all its rough heritage, is a gentle and earthy place. When a spectacular thunder and lightning storm stalled just off the coast not long ago, a large part of the town could be found on rooftops or sitting along the curb, applauding each new display of lightning and asking for encores. Yes, you might say people here are in touch.

While you are here—in addition to simply becoming part of this extraordinary place—there is almost a natural order of events for travelers. First, find a place to stay, either in Capitola or down by the waterfront. Next, check out Seaside Park and its rollercoaster. Have dinner and take a stroll on the pier or along the boardwalk. If it's summer, check out the Coconut Grove, a marvelous ballroom, right out of the '30s, featuring music from the period.

The following morning, go up into the big trees (with

a naturalist, if you can), have lunch at Roaring Camp, ride the steamtrain, then complete your drive through town. Anywhere else, that would be a heavy schedule. Here, it's somehow easy.

If you're a rollercoaster buff, of course, your eyes are already on the Giant Dipper.

This coaster opened to long lines of enthusiastic riders in 1924, and has been the centerpiece of the boardwalk ever since. Once again, as with portions of the Santa Monica Pier, the concept and its execution was the work of Arthur Loof, who imagined the coaster as a twisting ride that combining sensations of a balloon ascension, a drop from an airplane, and an earthquake.

After riding the Giant Dipper, serious coaster aficionados say that Loof is three for three on that one. And nearly fifty million riders over the years would agree.

In an age of rolling, swirling, inverted rides and drops—including one called the Vomitron—the Giant Dipper still reigns supreme. And why not? It is, after all, a Woodie, with the spidery look of something daring that is also sweet to behold in the bell-like curl and fall of its track.

Most important, it has a true coaster sound, from the clatter of the safety cog as you are drawn up the first incline slowly enough to have your heart at full race before the first drop. After that, there is a special resonance in the wooden timbers as the cars' wheels race over shining steel rails. Bottoming out after some of the steeper drops and curves is almost like riding a giant cello.

Loof's creation is a National Historic Landmark now and has brought thrills to riders for over seventy-five years. By any measure, the coaster is an out-and-out classic.

As you wait your turn in line, watching and listening to the cars roaring down from above and the shrieks of unbridled joy, the Giant Dipper becomes something of even greater value. It is proof that our childhood has not been lost—that we *can* go home again. And this is where you buy the ticket.

By contrast, the redwoods are almost surreal. And we came close to losing them all—only 3 percent of the original two million acres of California coast redwood forest remains uncut.

In 1867, Joseph Welch bought 350 acres of redwood forest in Felton, intending to log them. But his wife managed to convince him, that with a railroad coming, the trees might have more value as a tourist attraction. And was she right!

Even Teddy Roosevelt, along with thousands of European and U.S. visitors, came to the Welchs' resort. Today, that area is one of only two virgin groves left in the country. But these trees are more than beautiful and serene to the eye—they are living families, joined in an intimate and surprising fashion. And touring the grove with an inspiring naturalist can make all the difference.

Redwood Adventures offers tours of the great trees with such reverence you'd think you were tiptoeing through the Sistine Chapel—except that the chapel is once removed, and the redwoods are direct. Arrange for a tour (with a marvelous woods lady who redefines the word *energy* and can move hardened criminals to tears) that will change the way you think about the connections of nature. (831-338-1191)

Just out of Santa Cruz, you'll notice a leather company on your right. It was here that the Spanish settlers (Californios), with their high-born manners, silver saddles, and beautiful wives collided with American mountainmen, here to take out as many board feet of lumber as they could, and ship it to ports worldwide. The Californios were disgusted by the rough ways of the Americans, who in turn thought the settlers were too *la-de-da*. But the Californios wanted to sell beef and leather. The Yankees had big appetites, ships, and a tanning company. Silver crossed palms, bottles were uncorked, a deal was struck. The tannery is still here.

Into the Big Trees	Back to Santa Cruz
From Beach St., jog south onto West Cliff Dr., and turn right onto Bay St. At Mission St. (CA 1) turn right and continue onto a short freeway section, exiting northbound on River St., which becomes CA 9. Continue on to the entrance at Henry Cowell State Park on your right.	From Henry Cowell State Park, turn right on CA 9 and at the only traffic signal in Felton, turn right onto Graham Hill Rd. and continue on back to Santa Cruz. You may feel a bit turned around here, but don't fret, what you're doing is probably correct.

Parking is $5 at the grove. But after you've finished your tour, you can leave your car right where it is and amble on over to Roaring Camp & Big Trees Narrow-Gauge Railroad—perhaps the best of all such attractions—and walk in free.

The camp was established by Issac Graham, who built a distillery here, plus the first water-powered sawmill west of the Rockies—two things you'd better have if timber is your business. Californio families referred to this place as that "wild and roaring camp." The name stuck, and though the locale in Bret Harte's *Luck of Roaring Camp* was later changed to the Sierra foothills, this place provided the story's basis.

Roaring Camp is a great place to potter around, with a nice general store, plus a great pit BBQ and live country music. Not to mention a steam train ride through the redwoods on a narrow-gauge railway—of which there is a wonderful tale.

Narrow-gauge railways were built as an alternative to standard-gauge lines, which are 4 feet $8\frac{1}{2}$ inches exactly. But what is standard about that? As it happens, our early railroads were designed by British engineers. And their knowledge had come, in turn, from the adaptation of horse-drawn coaches to rail service—the wheels of which were 4 feet $8\frac{1}{2}$ inches exactly.

Why were the wheels such an odd distance apart? Because they had to fit in the permanent grooves that had been worked into roads over a thousand years before by the wheels of Roman chariots—which were exactly 4 feet $8\frac{1}{2}$ inches apart . . .

Back in Santa Cruz, or on your way out of town, be sure to take in the Surfing Museum at the lighthouse. It has a good collection, and overlooks one of the best surfing spots on the West Coast: Steamer Lane.

NORTHERN COAST

DAVENPORT-PACIFICA

On up CA 1, not far from Santa Cruz, is a delightful spot often missed by travelers but well-known to coasties and students. It's the town of **Davenport,** where you can find great browsing and a good meal—huevos rancheros or chili or curried tofu make good choices—for a nice price at the Cash Store, plus warmly hosted accommodations (see Lodging).

Davenport was once a whaling boomtown. A fire in 1915 wiped out everything except the town jail. Today its bluffs are a good place to watch migrating gray whales.

Potter around town for a bit, and pick up a muffin for the road. For there's a wonderful stop coming up at Año Nuevo State Reserve, known largely as a mating ground for the giant elephant seals who come ashore in December.

These magnificent animals—sometimes over twenty feet in length and weighing in at three tons or more—were hunted to near-extinction. With suitable protection, they have now come back from the brink. The reserve is also a wonderful place to walk a mile or so along self-guided trails, whether the seals are performing or not. Enjoy.

If Año Nuevo demonstrates how special places can be held in trust for the future, **Costanoa** is equally impressive as an environmentally responsible development.

Through a historic public-private agreement reached over ten years ago, both wilderness areas and farmland have been preserved along an unspoiled part of the coast that had been targeted for residential development.

Instead, a wilderness experience is offered those who have graduated from the ranks of day-long hikers. And for those who don't want a garage full of camping gear that finds use twice a year (maybe), Costanoa is a dream come true, and a sweet reminder of what camping in the grand style was like from the 1900s through the 1920s.

Watch for the understated entrance on the landward side of the highway two miles north of Año Nuevo. Here, you'll find a beautifully turned-out lodge, cabins, and remarkable tent bungalows: a real door, a real floor, but canvas over your head, just like the real thing. Plus a continental breakfast. Rates are $60–$240, or pitch your own tent here for a little less. (650-879-1100)

Some bath-and-shower facilities are shared, just like the state-park thing, but Costanoa supplies heated floors, sauna, central courtyard, and fireplace. All your camp songs will come up. And if S'mores don't do it for you anymore, head on up to the lodge for whatever you'd like. Oh, you'd like room service in your tent? You've got it!

Hiking, beachcombing, rental bikes; there's nothing lacking with over 30,000 acres of wilderness to choose from. Or maybe you'd just like to drive in and have a look around? Super. Pick up something from the General Store & Gourmet Deli and picnic right here on the grounds.

Costanoa is unique in almost every regard and is a sight—and an experience—not to be missed on this coast or in this life.

Three miles beyond Costanoa is Pigeon Point Lighthouse, one of the most beautiful and photogenic on any coast. Tours are available and midday or afternoon lighting work well.

Pigeon Point is also the first clue that the land-sea union is changing once again. Planted fields soon begin rolling down the hills and the shoreline is a preview of the rugged Mendocino coast, with rocky bluffs and miles of driftwood-covered beaches.

It's about a mile inland from CA 1, but **Pescadero** is worth that and more. Not much larger or smaller than it ever was, the town is host to Duartes (*Doo-arts*) Tavern. Hungry travelers have been making this a regular stop for years.

The place started out as a rough-plank bar, with one barrel of whiskey, in 1894 and was a solid success until Prohibition. In 1926, however, there was a major fire here. Quick-thinking firemen made sure the bar was saved. Today, it's the home-grown vegetables, plus artichoke soup and mountainman omelets, that packs 'em in. Be sure you're among them.

Back in Prohibition days, when places like Duartes Tavern were being closed, police-protected speakeasies were the rage. And the best combination for their suppliers was a protected cove or bay adjacent to a major market. **Half Moon Bay** was perfect.

Always an agricultural community, with a solid farm-town feel, Half Moon Bay has a charming Main Street—one block east of CA 1—with many originals.

This entire section of coastline has often been divided, with some eager for tourism, and many slow to embrace it. So, Half Moon Bay has preserved a good sense of itself.

About three miles north of Half Moon Bay, near Pillar Point, keep an eye out for Maverick's, the big-water surf center of the West Coast, with storm waves near forty feet.

Farther along the coast, you'll encounter sleepy **Moss Beach** and **Pacifica**—the last of the coastal towns that maintain an identity of their own. Stop for a latte and enjoy it. By the time you reach **Daly City,** you'll be freeway-bound and on the edge of citydom.

SAN FRANCISCO

If you were to recruit a cross-section of Californians, plus a measure of free-thinkers of every known preference, and asked them to design a city that satisfied all their needs, they would tell you to forget it—they already have one. It is San Francisco.

The city is not nearly so large as its reputation. Only forty-seven square miles, compared to five hundred square miles for Los Angeles. Still, its three-quarter million inhabitants make it the second-largest, and certainly the most interesting city in the Bay Area.

Californians can give endless reasons for loving San Francisco. But mostly it is because this place is so unlike the rest of the state. Neither sprawling nor sun-burned like the south; neither rural nor conventional like the north.

San Francisco has seasons and rains and fogs and mountainous streets and social agendas that can dismay visitors from anywhere. People don't just coexist here, they actually live together in a city able to celebrate the fact that the Chinese fortune cookie was actually invented by a Japanese-American gardener. And where else would you find a woman-owned porno shop, called Good Vibrations?

Of course, the city can sometimes be as haughty as it is entertaining. It is as cosmopolitan as New York without the raw edge, and as workable as Chicago without the wind and snow. In short, San Francisco is damn near a miracle.

So even if San Francisco (never Frisco) is in some respects an aging madam as critics have said, she is also an absolute beauty in her years. Still able to tickle your fancy in unexpected ways. And that—in this imperfect life—is as good as it gets.

You may already have your own agenda for San Francisco. But, if this is your first visit, a service like Cyndi Recommends (415-383-4505) can save you time and money on attractions that interest you most. It's like having your own concierge! And new self-guided tours are always being developed that roadies appreciate. Cyndi Recommends comes highly recommended.

PLANNING TIP: Before anything else, request a copy of the *San Francisco Book,* published by the San Francisco Convention and Visitors Bureau (415-391-2000). It's happy homework.

Also, if you're traveling south, a little backtracking will be necessary, but you'll be driving alongside Golden Gate Park, so think of that as an added benefit.

Northbound	Southbound
Continue northbound on CA 35 as it becomes Skyline Blvd. Turn left on Great Highway and continue north to Sutro Heights and Cliff House.	From Golden Gate Bridge, take CA 1 and turn right on Fulton St. Turn right again on Great Highway. Continue to Sutro Heights and Cliff House.

Cliff House is one of those magical sites that seems to have been part myth from the beginning. Travelers and locals—to say nothing of folks like the Crockers, Stanfords, and Hearsts—have been coming here since it opened in 1863. Today, Cliff House is in its third incarnation.

The first was sold to Adolph Sutro, a tireless promoter—and not inconsequentially, a millionaire—who brought the people out to his baths (the ruins of which are well worth exploring) by salting the pool bottom with $20 goldpieces. He even built his own railroad to serve the site, only to see fire destroy the structure.

Sutro not only rebuilt Cliff House, he fashioned it into an extraordinary eight-story palace in the style of a French château, which survived the earthquake of 1906, again to be destroyed by fire.

Today's Cliff House was built in 1909, renovated several times, and is now in the care of the National Park Service. It combines nineteenth-century charm, with a Deco feeling from the 1930s and '40s. The food and service are good, the view spectacular. Be sure to allow enough time to ramble about the place.

From Cliff House drive east and turn left on Legion of Honor Drive (at 34th). If you have never cared much for fine art, the Palace of the Legion of Honor is the very place to have a change of heart. Commemorating veterans of World War I, the Palace has recently been renovated and expanded. The museum's site above Golden Gate Bridge is spectacular in itself and virtually every exhibit is a show-stopper.

Continue north on El Camino del Mar to Lincoln Blvd. After passing under the Golden Gate approach, turn left on Long Avenue/Marine Drive to visit Fort Point.

This place is like a magnet to kids and filmmakers alike, and has had starring roles in more movies and television dramas than could be listed. One look at any photograph of the Golden Gate before the bridge was built explains Fort Point perfectly. There are knowledgeable docents, and you can even learn how to fire a cannon. Enjoy.

From Fort Point, continue on through the Presidio on Lincoln. You'll soon notice the colonnades of the Palace of Fine Arts on your left. That structure now houses the award-winning Exploratorium, which affords participants exciting opportunities to explore science, mathematics, weather, and more. Just follow the signs to parking.

Departing, continue east on Lombard Street. As long as you're in this part of the city, it's always a hoot to wiggle down the famous S-bends of this handsome street (Campers and trailers prohibited). Stay on Lombard for seven more blocks and turn right on Telegraph Hill Boulevard to visit Coit Tower, another of the city's most recognized movie backdrops. *Play It Again Sam,* among many others, was filmed here.

Ready for Fisherman's Wharf? If so, double back on Lombard to Powell and turn right. At Jefferson turn left, take any parking place you can and walk north. Then, if you need to walk off some of the goodies you've sampled, head five blocks west to the Maritime Museum, where you'll find vintage sailing vessels and other relics of a bygone era along the West Coast. Pier 39 is also a base for Seaplane Tours, a landmark—*air*mark, really—in San Francisco since 1945 (see Above the Coast).

From Fisherman's Wharf, you can also catch a great cable-car ride up Hyde Street, and from there take a Washington Street car over to the Cable Car Museum and viewing gallery, where the understreet part of the cable car system is on wondrous display.

Back on the waterfront, follow the Embarcadero southbound to Pier 45, footing Brannan Street, where you'll find SS *Jeremiah O'Brien.*

Of the 2,700 Liberty Ships built during World War II, just two remain. And only the *O'Brien* made it back to Normandy for the anniversary of D-Day—crossing the Atlantic in the tender care of men who had served aboard her fifty years before.

You can tour the *Jeremiah O'Brien* any day of the week. On the third week of each month, she runs up her triple-expansion steam engine—which appeared in the film *Titanic*—and in May and October, the grand old lady takes to the bay with passengers. A voyage not to be missed if you're in town.

And, of course, there is Chinatown. With the exception of the two Chinas across the Pacific, more Chinese live in this sixteen-block area than anywhere else. Chinatown is best done on foot with a knowledgeable tour guide from the Chinese Cultural Center or a similar tour.

A two-hour tour is a good start in discovering that Chinatown is a special window on an accomplished civilization—one that was already inventing the compass, paper, printing, and medicine at a time when the English were still painting themselves blue.

Remember, too, that you will be moving from a society where time is measured in minutes (or at most, quarterly earnings reports), into a culture where the rhythm of time is expressed in entire generations and hundreds of years. Most of us are strangers to that, and it takes a little getting used to.

Not much has seemed to change San Francisco—well, earthquakes, sure—over the years. The city passed through four wars as a major embarkation point, played host to millions of Shriners, and had its famous skyline threatened by an all-time ugly freeway, until the citizens and Mother Nature conspired to end such nonsense and bring the thing down.

Life in the city has not always gone well, of course. In 1934, San Francisco captured the world's attention with a general strike by labor. That infuriated city officials, who were little interested in the plight of laborers anyway. And the newspapers, long the bastion of truth (and daily advertising), went absolutely ballistic.

Fueled by William Randolph Hearst and his personal style of bear-baiting, what began as a peaceful demonstration over the deaths of two men at the hands of police, turned violent. Despite pleas by observers like Will Rogers, paid strikebreakers went free, while four hundred strikers were beaten and arrested.

But unlike other cities, San Francisco learned. And during the late 1960s, when the city played unwitting host to countless flower-children from all across the U.S., the kids (and their money, to be fair) were patiently welcomed.

Evenings in San Francisco are a panoply of diversion. Tony Bennett is sometimes in town and most every major entertainer turns up here regularly.

But if you've steamed the wrinkles out of your best duds and are looking for the perfect capper, head for California at Mason: Number One Nob Hill. That's the world-famous address of the superb Mark Hopkins Inter-Continental Hotel.

Built in 1926, the Mark Hopkins has been called architecturally perfect, and is as special as any place can be. It also happens to have rates that are reasonable (for San Francisco) and is far more than lodging for the night. You can also save with your Auto Club card. (415-392-3434) Mind you, even the AAA calls the Mark Hopkins *refined*. So dress jackets are in order.

From the truly regal lobby, take the elevator all the way up. There, the Top of the Mark is a splendid lounge, where perhaps more stories of love gained or lost have been spun out than in any other place in America. Polished wood, linens, a grand piano playing in the background, and a sense of perfect moment are what you'll find here—where traditions are thicker than bar tabs.

One of these is the Squadron Bottle, from which an airman could request a free drink—unless it was the last, in which case he was honor-bound to buy a new bottle.

This tradition has now been re-created for authors. If your book was published by a recognized house, bring a copy to sign for the hotel's permanent Herb Caen Bookshelf, and ask for the Author's Bottle. It is sixty-year-old Johnnie Walker Blue Label scotch, casked in the same year that the Top of the Mark was born. You'll find none better, but you are still on your honor. If it's the last drink, you're buying the next bottle!

The Top of the Mark was converted from penthouses in 1939 to a skylounge—with special plate glass to withstand the wind. And it is where wartime marriages (or thirty-day liaisons) began or ended in the 1940s and '50s. And again in the '60s.

From the northwest part of the room, called Weeper's Corner, is a perfect view of the Golden Gate. As their loved ones sailed off to war, women watched from here, clinging to the legend that doing so would bring a safe return home.

So when you visit, raise your first glass to the solemn promises made here—that despite all prayers and hope and courage—could not be kept.

Other spectacular views and lounges can be found in the city today, but none better. If you spend only one evening in San Francisco, let it end here at the Top of the Mark.

SAUSALITO–BODEGA BAY

There are several ways in and out of San Francisco, but only one true portal—the Golden Gate Bridge. With a main span of 4,200 feet, and the first to be painted in what is now known as International Orange, the bridge is a masterpiece from any viewpoint, and a testament to the resolve of Bay Area residents to do what's right.

Still, it wasn't easy. Plans and proposals were haggled over from 1916 to 1930 when plans were finally accepted and the job got underway. And what a job it was! Huge caissons, able to withstand a pounding from Pacific storms, had to be sunk for the tower bases. Cables and construction technology had to be developed as work progressed. For perhaps the first time, union workers were hired for their skills and not merely for standing up and work actually progressed ahead of schedule.

Still, the most heartening part of the entire effort was that, when it was announced that millions were needed to complete the bridge, tens of thousands of San Franciscans put up the mortgages on their homes to make sure the dream did not fail.

There are well-marked viewing areas with adequate parking on both sides of the bridge—with lighting being best on the San Francisco side in the morning, and on the Marin side in the afternoon. And crossing is inexpensive if you need a couple of tries. Northbound traffic pays no toll; southbound vehicles are nicked only three bucks.

All of which says nothing of the feeling of going out on this amazing span, with the Art Deco look of the towers and those mesmerizing cables. Walk or drive. And enjoy.

As you wind down from the bridge on US 101, you'll find several exits for **Sausalito.** This hillside enclave of artists and writers once defined bohemianism on the West Coast, with roots deep in the Greenwich Village culture. Visitors came over on weekends to see sidewalk displays and buy quite good art at off-gallery prices.

It was a good thing and many of the visitors soon opened hundreds of shops and restaurants, which was not such a good thing. Now a large part of the town misses being kitsch by *that* much.

DRIVER'S NOTE: If you have a van—or anything larger—and you are not experienced in mountain driving, the section of CA 1 between Sausalito and Bodega Bay may be ill-advised. The road is often narrow, with twisting off-camber turns that are great for sports cars, but aggravating for larger vehicles. You'll still be able to reach Mendocino by taking US 101 to the coast via CA 12 from Santa Rosa or CA 128 from Cloverdale. That said, press on.

For CA 1 north, keep a sharp eye out after exiting Golden Gate Bridge, for a traffic sign marking a left turn for Stinson Beach.

If you find yourself sometime later, in a lovely, tree-shaded village where women with legs that go on forever are walking small dogs, and everyone looks as though they have just returned from their personal trainers—which they probably have—you have missed the turn and are in Mill Valley.

Backtrack to the Golden Gate Bridge area and take another shot, it can happen to anyone (*blush*).

This beautiful drive up through Golden Gate National Recreation Area is unique. But your average speed will often be 35 mph or less across to the coast, and not much better as you continue north.

NAVIGATOR'S NOTE: From San Francisco, driving time to Mendocino is about three and a half hours—plus time for stops or congestion. So the Garberville area will be about it for the day, and you'll want to allow time for the giant redwoods (quite different from the coastal variety). Plan on Eureka for the next night or at the most, Smith River.

So it's best to approach this first section in a relaxed way, perhaps with a bagel and some juice. That way you'll better enjoy the beautiful stands of eucalyptus—an import from Australia, but not always a good friend here in fire season—and blue gum.

After a few miles, however, the forest simply stops and you'll find yourself moving through a hilly section reminiscent of the mountain canyons of Malibu, with stunning views of a polished blue-steel sea ahead near **Muir Beach.**

It's easy to become turned-about on this section. And there's a goofy junction with Muir Woods Road partway through. Ignore it, what you're doing is probably correct.

Olema gives the first indication that this entire region has given itself over to the Bay Area weekender market. From here through **Point Reyes Station, Marshall, Tomales,** and **Bodega Bay,** the towns are encrusted with SUVs—the modern counterpart to blundering '50s station wagons—and awash with visitors from nearby cities who have nothing to do and have come here to do it.

Near **Stinson Beach,** ocean vistas open up again, but the road is more exacting, and locals show no regard for centerlines. So regard any blind curve with skepticism.

There are any number of good restaurants along this wild-farm-citified stretch of Pacific Coast Highway, but your choice (unless you are traveling off-season) will be determined less by ratings than by wait-times for seating, often an hour or more.

If you love back bays and marshlands for the animal and birdlife they spawn, you'll be positively swivel-headed on the twelve-mile drive along **Tomales Bay.** Note, here, that the mountains rising above you to the east are quite different in character from those just across the bay.

That's because the mountains out there to the west really don't belong here. At the lance-tip of the great San Andreas fault that defines much of California, the mountains across the bay came from the south, and are being pushed north several inches per year as the great tectonic plates do their work.

During the 1906 San Francisco earthquake, the tip of land here slid north twenty-one inches in a few seconds. Imagine what would happen if Manhattan or Berlin or Paris took a ride like that.

JENNER–GUALALA

Jenner is villagelike in the way it is laid out, and dependent on the tourist draw of **Fort Ross,** once an outpost for Imperial Russia that became but another predictor of the czar's ultimate downfall. The fort is all the more interesting simply because it has little of the Daniel Boone look we've come to expect from our own structures of this period. It is certainly worth a visit.

At Jenner Inn and Cottages, there are reports of strange goings-on in Mill Cottage, an old Victorian built for the local miller. Unlike many tales involving the supernatural, there is no awesome event or tragedy to infect the imagination, or to make one willing to believe in ghostly retribution. Just disappearing images of children playing or a couple dancing or sensory annoyances—like a terrible odor that once gripped the place.

Over the years, notes have been kept by visitors to Mill Cottage of events that took place there. If you're an amateur ghostbuster, though, this is a good place to put your two cents in.

Along the highway, the coast has changed character again and seems intent on becoming almost totally desolate by the time Cape Mendocino is reached.

Coast dwellers have for years put up with a moneyed

influx of vacation-home builders who invariably have little regard for the look of a place and build some monstrosity of their own design. **Sea Ranch** is different. And if, to the untrained eye, the gray-sided structures appear to be the wreckage of a great condominium complex that crashed here, the pieces are at least uniform.

Many are also vacation rentals that go for around a thousand per week. If you have four or more in your party and want to spend more time here, it's a pretty good deal.

Farther along **Gualala** (*Wa-la-la*) is a looser but more individually stated collection of shops and homes, with a special attraction. St. Orres, a Russian Orthodox church now in service as a B&B, retains its domed splendor and is quite photogenic.

After another twenty miles of largely undisturbed coastline, **Point Arena** appears, looking like a bit of ceramic decoration. Sited on one of the most beautiful outcroppings along the California coast, the lighthouse and its surroundings are in every way magnificent. Whether you are a lighthouse buff or not, this is a worthwhile stop. You may recall the location from scenes in *Forever Young*, a fluff-film saved by a charming Mel Gibson. A fine little museum is also maintained at the station.

MENDOCINO–FERNDALE

Approaching Cape Mendocino, the coastal bluffs and coves are as desolate as they are scenic, and made all the more forbidding by the whale-slaughter that went on along this coast for so long.

New England–style homes and storefronts of clapboard and cedar shake dominate the architecture of **Mendocino** proper, giving the town a misplaced look of mystery. No wonder Alfred Hitchcock was attracted to the place, or that the long-running television series *Murder, She Wrote* was in part set here.

If you are an inveterate shutterbug, you may want to snap the *MSW* house at 45110 Little Lake Street, now a charming B&B. Otherwise head on down to the waterfront, where most of the Kodak moments are clustered.

It's also a good idea to park a few blocks away, and not even attempt to drive down Main Street, where everyone's preoccupation is finding, saving, losing, or safely exiting a parking place.

The town is wonderfully picturesque, but within a few minutes, you'll wonder whether all the people are here to see the town or simply to say that they did.

If you plan on staying overnight, there are a number of B&Bs, plus the Mendocino Hotel, right on Main Street.

But a far more charming—and instructive—place to stay or take a meal is the Stanford Inn at Comptche Ukiah Road, on the east side of CA 1.

Although the inn had been in operation for some years, it has bloomed and is in a constant state of re-creation and renewal under the Stanfords, its present owners. The inn grows virtually all its herbs, in a carefully tended garden, and many of its own vegetables. An indoor pool—de rigeur along the Mendocino coast—is really a self-contained tropical paradise of surprising invention.

The waterfront facility is extensive, with outrigger ca-noes for paddlers to catch the river's flood tide, returning with the current, altogether a delightful round-trip. There are also llamas on site, and the connection between this inn and its physical and spiritual environs is at the very least remarkable.

Shortly after a death in the family, as the new dining room was nearing construction, a pair of ravens moved into the California grand firs on the property, and in a surprising series of events demonstrated themselves to be protectors of a sort. Thus, the new dining room was named after them.

If you are unable to stay at the Stanford, the inn offers open dining for lunch and dinner. And you'll find everything, from the great fireplace to individual table settings, just as it is somehow supposed to be.

In all, from its superb vegetarian-intimate menu, to its studied place in its surroundings, the Stanford Inn reflects its owners in being self-reliant and environmentally con-nected. Room rates are $215 and up with a full-service breakfast included. Lunch and dinner prices are moderate for the area. It's a grand vision in a state that is often short-sighted. Enjoy. (800-331-8884)

Not all Native Americans along the West Coast were

so laid-back as the Chumash and other southern nations. **Fort Bragg** was built originally to contain any ideas of uprising on the Mendocino Reservation. When the reservation was moved, the army got out of the fort business. As elsewhere in this region, lumbering interests prevailed. The Skunk Railway—so-called because of the smell the engines gave off—recalls the days when any tree was fair game, with a forty-mile ride to Willits. A small fishing fleet still hangs its nets at Noyo Harbor, but as with much of the Northern California–Oregon coast, the fisheries are nearly gone.

Just north of Rockport, CA 1 turns inland and hangs it up. From here on, through Oregon and Washington, Pacific Coast Highway is typically numbered US 101.

LEGGETT–MYERS FLAT

When US 101, called the Redwood Highway in Northern California, was first opened as a roadway, that term expressed hopeful optimism. More than anything, it resembled the forest-cut roads of the Appalachians that gave rise to the Conestoga Wagons that could clear the stumps left in the center of the road. When it rained—and it can really rain up here—the road became a mire, and where no swamps existed before, the road created some.

But America is a nation of roadies, and we like a challenge. So attractions soon sprouted. The original Drive-Thru Tree, something of an institution, is just south of **Leggett,** and worth a drive through.

Farther north, through two groves of redwoods, lies **Benbow Valley.** Relatively unknown, even to Californians, this charming little sunspot enjoys an early spring and an Indian summer lasting well into October, rivaling New England's autumn colors.

It was here in 1926 that the Benbow family built their inn. Designed in an English Tudor style, the place has been embellished but kept true to its original form for seven decades. It is on the National Register, but more than that, reflects the grace and care of its present owners. Like tea and scones served on the terrace.

Each room is furnished with antiques, plus a basket of mystery novels and poetry, a decanter of sherry, plus coffee and tea service. The result is a quality that defines good innkeeping: on entering, despite the surrounding elegance, it feels just like home.

Reservations may be made by phone (707-923-2124) or on the Internet, which is a blessing to the owners. When many guests who have heard of the inn telephone for reservations, the owners are tired of explaining that it is not the Bimbo Inn, but something a bit more sedate.

It's been a while since the last major marijuana bust around **Garberville,** which is all right with the town. Redwoods are really the main attraction here. Well-stocked with motels, Garberville is at the southern entrance to the Avenue of the Giants, a beautiful drive through the big trees. **Myers Flat** is at the northern edge. Either offers excellent access.

RIO DELL–EUREKA

At the southern approach to **Rio Dell,** sections of old US 101 appear. For roadies and those (including yrs trly) who cannot resist photographing spidery old bridges, the Scotia exit will lead you right to it. Scotia itself is the last of the wholly owned company towns of the lumbering era and its landlord, the Pacific Lumber Company, offers a splendid self-guided tour of the world's largest sawmill. Passes are available at the museum in town. The historic Scotia Inn is now being operated as a B&B, so you might want to check it out.

On up the road, along a stretch of old US 101, **Fortuna** advertises itself as a friendly city, and certainly seems to be. Although the south end of town is overrun with franchises, restoration and adaptive reuse is evident farther north, prompted no doubt by the great success of **Ferndale,** which cast its eyes on Mendocino's early success, and thought: *we can do that.* And it has. In the studied way that some towns discover the drawing power of words like *historic* and *quaint,* Ferndale is what so many other tourist towns could have been and are not.

Ferndale's main street is virtually franchise-free, and it retains an essential farm-bureau quality that entirely fits the place. Moreover, new construction around town carefully echoes the period look of downtown—with none of the false attempts at authenticity seen elsewhere.

Some may complain that any level of tourism brings ruin to a local culture. The answer is that, without tourism, many of these architectural treasures would have disappeared. Or worse, be covered in aluminum siding.

Ferndale is well worth the short detour from US 101, and a drive-thru tour. Don't miss the Shaw House and the Victorian Inn Hotel on Main Street, or the exquisite Gingerbread Mansion Inn at 400 Berding Street.

On Humboldt Bay, to the north, **Eureka!** hews just as closely to its heritage, and still makes room for growth. Indeed, at a time when the phrase *best-kept secret* has become a cliché, Eureka surpasses nearly every expectation. No wonder local publications use an exclamation point. Eurekans are also quick to remind us that it is the only city name to appear on the Great Seal of the State of California. And, yup, it is.

This is a gem of a town, with carefully planned redevelopment programs, and strong support from residents. And it is clearly a work-in-progress.

But little can be seen from the divided sections of US 101. Instead, here is a scenic route through town.

Northbound	Southbound
Exit US 101 at Herrick Ave. and turn right, following Herrick up the hill as it curves left. Continue as Herrick becomes F St. At Harris, turn right. Continue to I St. and turn left. This will take you through the best of the renovated Victorians downtown and up to Old Town Eureka. Park at the Plaza, 2nd and E Sts. for unequalled photo opportunities. US 101 will be on your right only a couple of blocks away.	Exit US 101 at Old Arcata Rd./Sunnybrea and curve back over the freeway. Continue on Old Arcata Rd. about 7 miles as it becomes Myrtle Ave. Cresting a hill, turn left on Hall Ave. and continue until it bends sharply to the right and becomes Harris St. Continue on Harris to I St. and turn right. Continue on I St. through the renovated Victorians downtown and on into Old Town Eureka. Park at 2nd and E Sts. for photography, and rejoin US 101 to the southeast.

Whether you're a dyed-in-the-gingerbread Victorian fan or just discovering this one-hundred-year-old legacy, you'll want to spend time with Eureka's rich variety. There are more Victorians here per capita than in any other California city—10,000 in all. So if you're a fan, Old Town and the stunning Carson Mansion are just a beginning. Pick up self-guided touring information at the Chamber of Commerce, 2112 Broadway.

And if the thought occurs that absolutely none of these beautiful old-timers was built with power tools, you'll want to visit a truly unique place, the Blue Ox Millworks, at the foot of X Street. Not only is it a nineteenth-century sawmill created from tooling salvaged from scrap heaps, it is a school and a partnership in the preservation of working history—Victorian gingerbread throughout the Northwest can be duplicated here.

Stand in the gallery and marvel at a seventeen-foot lathe or the ease with which pickets can be cut in one swipe. Or take a walk out back to meet Babe and Blue, the ox-team, and a lumber-camp cabin built on skids, so that it could be moved at a moment's notice. After only a few minutes, you'll realize what a privilege it is just to be here.

One of the things we all learned from Paul Bunyan stories is that loggers have *huge* appetites. One way to find out how big is to make a two-for-one visit to the Samoa Cookhouse, across the Samoa Bridge (CA 255). Here you'll not only find a nineteenth-century cookhouse with original tables from 1872, but you can pull right up to one of those long tables and order a meal that will keep on coming until you call it quits! Great breakfasts, meatloaf like Mom wishes she made, and all the trimmins'. Looking out on the river, you'd expect Mark Twain to stroll up any minute and try to steal your dessert.

Eureka is one of the few cities to blend a sharply contrasting history with the present—and win. The place deserves its exclamation point!

ARCATA–SMITH RIVER

Imagine what would happen if the laid-back dudes and chicks of Santa Cruz all decided to wear heavier clothes and more hair, and you'll have a near-perfect image of **Arcata,** home to aging—and commercially successful— hippies, plus the Humboldt campus of California State University. Buildings on the campus were, when first finished, colored a bilious green, earning the school the nickname Jolly Green Giant, and attracting the sandal-and-bong set from all over the coast.

Yet for all its lightheartedness, Arcata is not frivolous. There's an amazing project in town that warrants a visit from travelers. It's the wastewater reclamation project. No kidding. If you were around during the 1960s and '70s or are attracted to Green ideals, make this a destination point, as do community planners from coastal regions throughout the world. From US 101, exit on westbound Samoa Boulevard and drive south toward the bay.

Instead of smelly concrete wash-pits, Arcata's wastewater is brought here, where Mother Nature does the laundering—and creates in the process a vast area of walkable wetlands that provide sanctuary for countless species of birds and water creatures. It's what we all hoped once to see. And here it is.

Now and then a town comes into view that seems as familiar as an old dream. **Trinidad** is like that. Just driving up the main street from the US 101 exit slows the heart a bit on the way to the memorial lighthouse and Trinidad Head beyond.

The town has a rich history in which waterfront interests mixed with Yurok tribal heritage to produce a curious independence that infuses the town to this day.

You can experience that firsthand at the small museum behind Ocean Wave Quilt Shop at 490 Trinity Street, or stop in at Trinity Art catty-corner across the street.

Seasons, almost totally absent farther south in California, give both a rhythm and a chronology to this place. And Yurok lore mixes its own presence. Down on the beach you're likely to find a sizeable log that an old Yurok, Humpback Jim, once decided to make into a canoe back in the early 1900s. But Jim died before he could finish the job, and each winter when the storms come, the log moves to a different spot, hoping perhaps to meet up with Jim again and get the job finished.

A lovely loop of old highway lies along Scenic Drive south of Trinidad and Stagecoach Road to the north. Northbound, take Westhaven exit from US 101. Southbound, exit at Patrick's Point or Seawood Drive. And set your watch back about a century.

From Trinidad north, you'll also notice that the offshore rock sentinels (called *seastacks*) are often crowned with trees, while to the south, they are barren.

On the Klamath River you'll drive over the Golden Bear Bridge—with its matching set of *really* golden bears—and it's just a preview of the magnificent bridges found along Pacific Coast Highway in Oregon. **Klamath** is a good place to get a sense of what happens to the cultural geography of the Pacific Coast while driving north.

In Southern California, the beach and its culture is certainly the main focus of coastal communities. Along the Central Coast, the beach recedes and the focus becomes the ocean. It remains that way through Southern Oregon. Then, the rest of the way north, even the ocean begins to recede, to become a backdrop for trees.

Just north of Klamath you'll find Trees of Mystery, one of the few remaining tourist attractions of its kind. Paul Bunyan is just an opener, the real stars are the trees themselves. Well worth the stop.

A little farther along, just a few miles south of **Crescent City,** you'll pass through a portion of Jedediah Smith Redwoods State Park, which is surprisingly beautiful for being right on a main highway, with a feeling of near-privacy about the drive through. This is also the location used in *Star Wars,* where Luke Skywalker and his chums all flew through the big trees.

And you can easily imagine the mind of a master filmmaker at work. The location is set, most of the characters are well developed by now. But what shall we call the wise ones, the ones so much like redwoods themselves? Another look at the map. Hmm. Jedediah Smith Redwoods. Well, how about *Jedi?* Works for me . . .

If, as you approach Crescent City, the place seems oddly open and uncrowded, it's because a major part of the city was flattened in 1964 by a tsunami—no longer called tidal waves, because they have little to do with tides—triggered by an earthquake in the Aleutian Islands.

Few understood tsunamis at the time or were aware that these waves extend thousands of feet below the ocean's surface and move at jet-aircraft speeds. Near land, shelving of the sea floor forces the waves to peak, anywhere from twenty to one hundred feet, while packing terrific force.

Crescent City has since rebuilt, of course. It is such a pleasant area, no one really wanted to leave. Follow a loop along Front Street to the Crescent Lighthouse Museum and return via the scenic drive on Battery/Howe Drive, flanking Beachfront Park.

Of course, wherever there are waves, you'll find surfers, and Crescent City is home to an annual longboard competition sponsored by Rhyn Noll Surfboards. One would only hope that no one here will try to ride the Big One.

If your road-food alert is sounding, it's because you're close to the Continental Bakery at 503 L Street, which is southbound US 101. From northbound M Street, turn left at Sixth Street and slide on into the parking lot at the back. Get there early, the locals do.

Smith River is the kind of place that has little reason for being, except it keeps attracting travelers who like the feeling, or the fishing, so much that they simply stay on. Time runs on a slow clock around here.

Which makes a sign of effort and ingenuity stand out all the more. For as you're driving along, you'll suddenly find a full-sized vessel, apparently tied up along the highway's edge—a museum, gift shop, and major advertising for Ship Ashore Resort—all in one.

The ship itself is a one-hundred-fifty-six-foot luxury yacht, built for a New York sugar tycoon by Krupp Iron Works in Kiel, Germany. And it cost close to a million in uninflated 1925 dollars. And it was fun while it lasted, but in 1942 the yacht was pressed into service as a patrol boat. After the war, the ship was brought to Smith River where it served as a floating restaurant and lounge. Ship Ashore's present owners placed her where she is today.

Even better is that Best Western Ship Ashore is a grand place to stay, to eat, to walk the beach, and to loaf. After you've negotiated the speed bumps (which are truly malevolent) and reached the motel, a sense of how nice it is around here begins to sink in: ocean-view rooms, with close-up bird-watching—a flock of Canadian geese have taken up residence—and a very nice restaurant and lounge. The property is family-owned and well managed. Can't do much better. Rates are from $58. (707-487-3141)

OREGON

If California and Washington have chafed against their isolation on the western side of the Rockies, Oregon has relished it. Perhaps, through early experience with the promoters of the Oregon Trail, people here learned that advertising is not necessarily a good thing.

There's also a solid midwestern feel about Oregon, in her residential architecture and small businesses, and in her politics. Even over life-and-death issues that would bring California politicians out swinging, Oregonians are more likely to come out grudging. Politics here is not a profit-center, but more something to be endured and mastered if the quality of life is to remain high.

And high it is. Smog and gridlock and gangland turf is all but unknown throughout most of Oregon. But not all, and that is keeping the kettle on the boil.

As in California and Washington, the ideals of preservation and the self-interests of commerce are often in headlong conflict here. And that has meant Jobs versus Environment. At least that's the spin most politicians feel most comfortable with. And why not? Spotted owls and trees don't vote. So therein lies a problem that Oregonians must struggle with for decades to come.

What's important to know, as we cruise along this magnificent coast and through the forests of this marvelous place, is that the path Oregon takes will likely affect us all in ways we cannot imagine. What we can offer, as this state confronts difficult issues, is our support and our patience.

Oregon's people, and the bounty of nature still to be found here—from forests to surfing beaches—deserve no less.

SOUTHERN COAST

BROOKINGS-BANDON

It's difficult to conjure an image of the lovely green-forested area around **Brookings** as a high-profile military target, but that's exactly what it became during the early days of World War II.

Embarrassed (and thereby infuriated) by Jimmy Doolittle's raid on Tokyo from the deck of the Navy carrier *Hornet,* the Japanese High Command searched for a way to strike directly against the Continental U.S.

The shelling of Ellwood Terminal had obviously not gone well, and an attack on a major coastal city like L.A. or San Francisco would risk a force of several carriers—or so the Japanese believed, not knowing that our coastal defenses were shooting at our own interceptors, which were often busy trying to shoot one another down.

The Imperial Japanese solution turned out to be very

much like one dating back to the early American West. Namely, if you can't win in a straight shoot-out with somebody, burn the guy's barn down.

So a Japanese seaplane pilot and his observer were hustled aboard a two-thousand-ton fleet submarine and sent off to bomb Oregon.

The idea was to set fire to the vast timber resources of the Northwest, which, coincidentally, were undefended. The resulting conflagration would both harm and frighten the pants off the West Coast. Still, for all its planning, the mission missed its mark.

The Yokosuka E14Y1 Glen floatplane carried but two small bombs, and the pilot seemed unsure of his headings. Of course, there was lots of forest to choose from. But the weather simply wasn't favoring forest fires at the time.

When the bombs were dropped from eight thousand feet, the pilot banked hard and returned to the sub. And though subsequently bombed by a pursuing American aircraft, the Japanese attackers made good their escape. On the U.S. mainland, the score was still Home Team—0, Visitors—0. Stay tuned, though, this one is a doubleheader.

Aside from a predictable spy scare, which the FBI itself loosed on the population, the attack did have one long-lasting effect on the West Coast. Residents of southern Oregon decided to end their secessionist movement toward a brand new state called Jefferson and join ranks with their brethren in the north, at least for the duration of the war. That union, happy to say, is still working.

Today, Brookings is as peaceful as it was in the early autumn of 1942. And it's the southernmost of several "Banana Belt" towns, in which the weather is said to be California-like, with few heavy storms, and pleasant year-round temperatures.

When the weather is good, Brookings also offers fine conditions for surfing and bodyboarding at Sporthaven Beach.

Just two miles north of town is Harris Beach State Park, one of the most carefully designed camping and day-use facilities to be found anywhere. Most parks are now so crowded that any feeling of being even semi-alone at a campsite is disappearing. But not here. In-season reservations are crucial, however.

CAMPING NOTE: Campsites may be reserved from anywhere in the world up to eleven months in advance for *both* Oregon and Washington at www.prd.state.or.us. If you plan on doing much camping along Pacific Coast Highway in the Northwest, this web site is certainly the place to begin.

A bit beyond Harris is Samuel Boardman State Park, stretching for ten miles along the coastline. And for some vague meteorological reason, even when beaches to the south and north are socked-in, the fog blows through here, clearing off earlier.

Farther along this beautiful stretch of coastline, the landforms change again, with new-growth forests creeping right up to the road. You'll also encounter one of the highest bridges in Oregon along this stretch, but since it is often impossible to see very far down, it may not matter.

It should be pointed out, in Oregon's favor however, that all along the coast—in summer especially—from San Diego north, fog is about a fifty-fifty affair. Whenever the heat builds throughout the inland valleys, the marine layer comes ashore, without as they say, fear or favor. And the more heat, the deeper the layer. So if you're making this drive under a five-thousand-foot deck of low clouds and fog, take some comfort in knowing that people in California are probably driving with their lights on, too.

For photographers, the seastacks just south of **Gold Beach** are truly remarkable and these sentinels line up perfectly for the lens in the morning.

And yes, gold really was found in the dark sands of this area. Way back when, at least. Now the gold is in the form of tourist dollars, and this area has plenty to offer. In terms of sheer popularity, jet boat trips up the Rogue River top the list. Choose between Jerry's Rogue Jets or Rogue River Mail Boat Trips. Either one is a thrill.

Farther along, on the west side of US 101, find a true charm from the past: Prehistoric Gardens. Even in fog you won't miss it, and it's one of those nutty places from the 1950s that help complete any touring experience— an old-time Jurassic Park, frozen in cement and the quirky vision of its creator.

A few miles south of Port Orford, you'll practically bump into Humbug Mountain, which is about the tallest thing on the Oregon coast, at close to two thousand feet. Rain or shine this mountain seems to have a curious effect on the weather and the drive-by is really quite striking.

Near **Port Orford,** you might have a shot at becoming a millionaire, if you want to hang around for a while. Things do have a way of falling out of the sky around here. Like a ten-ton meteorite that slammed into the Siskiyou National Forest just a few miles from here.

Every year treasure-hunters saddle up to search for the thing. The problem is no one has good directions anymore. Place-names have been changed, and original documents may have been deliberately altered, but the salient fact is—it's still out there somewhere, of almost incalculable value, and you'll have a lot better chance than with a state lottery.

Recall the Japanese submarine and the pilot who dropped two incendiary bombs on the forest near Brookings? Well, they turned up here, too . . .

After lying off the Oregon coast for the better part of a month, the submarine again launched its scout plane at the U.S. mainland, this time at a grassy area of unknown strategic importance in Port Orford. But the pilot was undone by his own home front. Both bombs were duds.

Still the mission had done what it could and all hands returned to the Home Islands. In 1962, the pilot returned to Oregon as a guest and handed over his Samurai sword, explaining that the highest pledge of friendship is to hand over one's sword of honor to a former enemy.

Although the story is still told in Port Orford, the city itself was best known for famed (and increasingly rare) Port Orford cedar—of which the Hotel del Coronado in San Diego was partially built—and as the coast's only open-sea port.

Port Orford is another Banana Belt town, with a mild climate. But when pressed, locals will admit that they do have horizontal rain here. That's when Pacific storms come ashore with such force that it is difficult to walk upright, and US 101—at some distance from the ocean—actually has seafoam blowing across it.

About ten miles north of Port Orford is Cape Blanco, said to be the westernmost point in the lower forty-eight, and another lighthouse for buffs and photographers— Oregon's oldest, dating from 1870.

Some places just seem to come by their charm naturally. **Bandon-by-the-Sea** is one of them. For one thing, the town is visually more open than others. And the union between town and seashore is more subtle and agreeable than elsewhere.

From the south, there is a nice drive along the shore. Watch for Beach Loop Road and signs for the state parks. The loop will conveniently deposit you at Old Town, which is worth exploring because it's so well done. Bandon is nicely supplementing its fading timber and fishery industries with conservative growth in tourism and technology-based small businesses. And Bandon Dunes is a world-class golf resort with an astonishingly beautiful course. Cottages and rooms at the clubhouse begin around $100.

Bandon has one of the most scenic—and extensive— beaches for walking or running that you'll find on the Oregon coast, and is a beauty for those Kodak (or Fuji) moments. If you're beginning to get a case of car fever, a stop for a little exercise might be just the ticket, and Bandon a good place. And don't put the cameras away before you check out the one-of-a-kind lighthouse in Bullards State Park, just across Coquille River.

Continuing north, you may not recognize the importance of this area to American tradition and your very own Thanksgiving dinner. For this is the major league of cranberry growing, and Bandon celebrates it with a passion at the annual Cranberry Festival the second week in September.

A perennial crop, with some granddaddy beds still in production after one hundred years, Oregon is chief supplier to the world, with crop values of about $10 million. And because cranberries are fairly fussy, they are best grown in a balanced ecological setting that also offers safe habitats for large numbers of local and migrating birds. Most cranberry bogs are virtually inaccessible, but there is a viewing point just off US 101 at Randolph Road.

COOS BAY–REEDSPORT

Like many harbor areas along the Oregon coast, the cities of **Coos Bay** and **North Bend** have been dealt a triple blow, forests and fisheries largely worked out, plus a dip in the export market.

Yet these Siamesed cities remain two of the most vibrant and interesting in Oregon. Not liberal by any means, the people here are true to traditional values. Still, the slowdown has cost many dockworkers their jobs and the region is scrambling to reshape the economy.

Along the southern approach to Coos Bay—the largest natural deep-water port between San Francisco and Puget Sound—you may see freight cars that have been tagged by some of the best graffiti artists in the Northwest. Officially, this is a no-no. Unofficially, the locals admire the work and do little to discourage it.

Through town, US 101 northbound is Bayshore Drive, while Broadway, a block west, carries southbound traffic.

International flags on the bayside of the highway line the waterfront boardwalk, and if you'll be staying over, there are charming dinner cruises aboard the *Rendezvous*.

Family-owned restaurants, where friendly service and good food go hand in hand, are a rarity these days, especially a mom-and-pop diner that floats. The owners—he's a shipwright by trade and she works with disabled children—built the bay cruiser in their backyard and have their hearts and souls in every foot of her. They also offer bay cruises. Just the story of their ark is worth the price of admission.

On the west side of the one-way highway through town, watch for the Coos Bay Visitor Information Center between Anderson and Commercial. As travelers' sources go, this center is excellent and most helpful with local and coastal information—and there's a brand new Coos Historic Museum being completed just to the north.

Or if you're ready for a little coffee, the Kaffe 101, next door, is a good place, with excellent baked goods. A memorial for Steve Prefontaine, a quadruple record-holder in the 10K, and one of this country's greatest runners, is also at the Center.

Coos Bay was once one of the busiest harbors on this

coast, as lumber-loading equipment gives testament. Now, adaptive reuse finds a home here. One need not be a gambler to appreciate the effort that turned a decaying shed into the Mill Casino.

The Bay Area is also the unofficial myrtlewood capital. This wood, with its subtle shadings, is endlessly fascinating to many—sort of like blue glass. In North Bend, as a matter of fact, money actually grew on trees, because myrtlewood was issued as legal tender during the depression—and is still redeemable.

The Oregon Connection, at 1125 S. First Street, offers a free factory tour. Travelers are often informed that this myrtle grows only in Oregon and the Holy Land. If the truth be known, however, this famous wood from the Oregon coast is actually *Umbellularia californica*—California laurel, which even grows in Bakersfield. Basically, it's the same tree that provides bay leaf for soups and stews. But hats off to the marketeer who branded the laurel as Oregon myrtlewood, creating an entire tourist industry.

North Bend was once slyly invited to become part of Coos Bay, and declined. Good thing, too. For the city never would have commissioned the bridgelike neon sign—last of its breed in Oregon—that has been suspended above US 101 since 1936.

Once a city composed almost entirely of saloons, bawdy houses, and churches catering to lumberjacks—some repentant, some not—North Bend is now a quiet community and southern anchoring point of the McCullough Bridge. But before driving over that magnificent bridge, here is a story of goodwill honored and remembered.

Virtually lost in American history was the visit of a French train made up of *40 et 8* boxcars—so-called because in World War I, each could carry forty men and eight mules. It was called the *Merci* Train.

At the close of World War II, the hearts of the French people were so filled with gratitude that, as a special train crossed France, thousands of French families, most made destitute by the war, brought out what heirlooms, medals, and precious items they had and carefully packed them aboard the train as a thank-you to American families who had given France their sons, and after the war, clothing and food.

Much was made of the *Merci* Train when it finally arrived in Oregon from New York. Its artifacts were taken into the public trust and then, unaccountably, forgotten by nearly every curator except those in the Bay Area. Here, they are proudly displayed at the Coos County Historical Society Museum, 1220 Sherman Avenue.

Along with glassware, a child's stuffed dog, and a plate is a letter from a family in the Oise region. In part, it reads: ". . . this little plate came from the mother of my grandmother. We apologize for not giving something more beautiful but what we give, it comes from the bottom of our hearts." And so shall it remain in ours. *Merci*.

Now, onto the McCullough Bridge. Completed in 1936, the structure is one of the most beautiful of Conde McCullough's designs, giving ample clearance to ocean-going vessels. And if you're on a roll with lighthouses, you'll want to watch for Umpqua Light and Discovery Center at **Winchester Bay.** Take the shoreline loop south of Salmon Harbor.

Throughout this entire area, from North Bend onward, you'll be in serious dune-buggy country. If you've never driven or ridden the dunes, it's an experience!

But do a little homework first at the Oregon Dunes Visitor Center in **Reedsport** on the west side of the highway at Umpqua Avenue. These dunes are magnificent, and knowing something about how they were created—and how fragile the dunes are—can add immeasurably to your ride.

CENTRAL COAST

FLORENCE–NEWPORT

Just south of **Florence** you'll come upon Honeyman State Park, which includes three lakes in its five hundred acres, and great care in providing wheelchair access to both trails and the lake. Roads and facilities within the park have been recently upgraded and it remains one of the most beautiful in Oregon.

If Florence itself was once beautiful, it has nearly lost its battle to the taco-mall look. Or perhaps the real Florence has simply been hidden away somewhere. But even this impression of the town is saved by another Conde McCullough bridge, which only seem to become more and more impressive as you drive north along the coast.

Old Town is being more carefully developed, with strong city design codes in place. Turn right a few blocks north of the bridge on Nopal, then make another right on Bay Street. There are several nice places to eat along Bay Street, and all the way to the west is the River House Motel, which makes a fine bookend for the area.

Eleven miles north of Florence and thirty-eight miles south of Newport, you'll find Sea Lion Caves. It's important to be fairly precise about this, because you'll be coming around a blind curve—and suddenly, there it is. Northbound, it's a surprise; southbound, the first indication you'll have is brakelights ahead as everyone scrambles off the road.

Now, this attraction is not for the faint of nose. There are no Porta-Pottis for sea lions and the caves are pretty well closed in. But this is also one of the grand old attractions along the West Coast.

Hecata Head is next, a beautiful spot, with what is perhaps America's most photographed lighthouse. Another neat thing about stopping here is that you get a free bridge as part of the deal. Fine shots of this historic bridge present themselves, and even in cloud, it is outstanding.

And just a bit farther is Cape Perpetua, undoubtedly one of the most striking landforms anywhere along the West Coast. Above, the small stone WPA shelter was used as a lookout point in World War II. Below, wave action eroded the rock here to such an extent that major blow-holes and caves have been created. If the tide is coming in strongly, this is a real treat for travelers with video cameras and a good rain hat.

A small community of some six hundred, **Yachats** (*Ya-hots*) takes some exploration to gain any sense of the town. Start with the visitor center on US 101 at 2nd Street. Ask about the little log church while you're there. And if you are in love with Oregon's coastline by now, stop in at Shirley's Cottage Industries, at 302 Coast Highway, Suite 2, for a look at large-scale posters featuring aerial views of this section of the coast—plus dome-dandy lighthouse art.

Waldport, straddling the Alsea River, with sandy beaches trailing off into rocky shoreline, is another fisherman's paradise, with lots of words like *landing* to tip you off. Or there's Fishin' Hole Trailer Park to really make the point.

In **Newport** the forces for good in roadside tourism are succeeding. Newport is home to the Oregon Coast Aquarium, Nye Beach, two lighthouses, and yet another graceful bridge.

If you're still in the planning stages and are reading this at home, you may be wondering about all the bridge-fuss. But once on this highway, you'll realize what treasures these WPA Conde McCullough bridges are. In an age when building, like almost everything else, is reduced to being the most universal and cheapest to produce,

McCullough's spires and curves are a treat beyond description.

Oregon Coast Aquarium is a marvel of community planning and was the rehab home of Keiko, the orca star of *Free Willy*. The aquarium is certainly one of the best in the country, and whether you missed the big tank in Monterey or are just a dedicated fishie, this is a fine exhibit. Located on the south side of the river, east of the highway, on Ferry Slip Road.

Beginning at the south end of town, there's the Bayfront district, with curiosities aplenty. But none reflect the 1930s and '40s more than *Ripley's Believe It or Not!* in Mariner Square at 250 SW Bay Boulevard, reached on the east side of US 101 via Canyon Way.

On the west side of the highway, you'll find Yaquina Bay State Park and Lighthouse. A lovely picnic place, with great photos and tales of hauntings for dessert.

Partway through town, turn left at Olive Street for Newport's Historic Nye Beach area along Coast Street and NW Beach Drive. This is a remarkable and very cozy-feeling enclave of artists and shopkeepers dating to the 1900s, when it was a fashionable seaside resort.

Soon, with hot baths and summer classes for college students, Nye Beach had become a center for learning, and retains that character today. Bookstores, quaint shops, excellent restaurants—you can enjoy High Tea here in a former theater—and homey B&Bs dot this area.

It is heartening to see such dedication to renovation and development. Nye Beach is a town on the comeback trail. Well worth some strolling time.

North of Newport, watch for Lighthouse Drive, leading to Yaquina Head Lighthouse and Natural Area. A terrific spot for tidepooling (wheelchair accessible), photography, and generally being in Oregon!

DEPOE BAY–LINCOLN CITY

Depoe Bay, which bills itself as the world's smallest harbor, also has a good how-we-got-our-name story. A member of the Siletz tribe worked here at the U.S. Army Depot. Well, he got to calling himself Charlie Depot and the name—though with an unaccountable spelling—

stuck. We are not told, however, why the town wasn't named Charlic.

Nor do we know whether the story is even remotely true. Because one look at this town will tell you that folks around here don't mind putting you on a little. There's Fuddy Duddy Fudge, Incorporated, and Gracie's Sea Hag, where "seafood is so fresh the ocean hasn't missed it yet." And there are also several inns and condo rentals in Depoe Bay that are stunning.

But the future is arriving with a jolt. In an area with beach homes available under $180,000, a new development is offering condos as one-month vacation rentals for $39,000 and up. Do the math and you'll see why some folks here are worried about the bust after every boom.

A few miles to the north, **Gleneden Beach** is home to world-famed Salishan Lodge and Golf Links, now owned by Westin and beautifully renovated. This was the first Oregon course to cooperate with the Audubon Society in providing sanctuary for birds, and if you haven't seen the course, it's a knockout.

Lincoln City was formed from several smaller communities and has filled in the blanks with some of the most aggressive development to be seen on the coast. Best known for bringing in Oregon's largest factory outlet mall, Lincoln City set the tone for other beach areas hurt by fading natural resources. Predictably, the town's character is changing from seaside center to shopper's resort. But you can still find charm here by looking a little. Check in with the Chamber of Commerce on US 101 at Logan.

And if you're doing a little novice surfing or bodyboarding, give the waves near Otter Rock a try. Elsewhere on Lincoln City beaches, the waves tend to be much heavier, and there's a good bit of localism.

Above bustling Lincoln City, **Neskowin** is a study in contrast. This is the kind of place you might wish your favorite granny lived in, so that you could come here to visit. It's tiny, only a few blocks, and fifteen miles an hour would be almost too fast, but if you want to get a sense of what it *could* be like to live here on the Oregon coast, this is a wonderful place to find that feeling.

NORTHERN COAST

Tillamook–Cannon Beach

A few miles beyond Neskowin, US 101 swings inland. A mile or so past Oretown, a left turn will take you on a seaside loop through **Pacific City** (where dorymen still launch their boats in the surf, and novice surfers are in good company) and **Oceanside,** where *Spitfire Grill* was filmed. This is Three Capes Drive, and unless it is exceptionally foggy, worth every minute.

Inland, the town names sing a different song, with Cloverdale and Beaver announcing that this is farm country again. And **Tillamook,** known for its namesake cheese, is a down-to-basics community.

But for aviation buffs, World War II historians, and travelers looking for the unusual, Tillamook has it all at the Naval Air Station Museum. Housed in a former blimp hanger one thousand feet long and covering seven acres, you will find one of the best collections of vintage aircraft to be seen anywhere in the world—and a story of sheer dedication.

For this extensive collection is privately owned by a man who loves old airplanes and shares his passion. The owner, whose name appears coincidentally on a Mini-Guppy outside the hangar, specializes in helicopter logging and construction, with worldwide experience in selective logging in environmentally sensitive areas.

Now these classics represent a major personal and

community asset. The museum is a treat, from the spot-less gift shop—with comfortable furnishings and space to relax over a cup of coffee—to the displays themselves. There's even an Air Base Cafe.

Still, nothing compares with the look on a grandchild's face or the expression in a wife's eyes as a gray eagle talks about how, when he was young, he flew one *like this.*

As you leave, be sure to take a quick peek at the dam-aged left wing of the converted Boeing 377. It happened when a wind came up one day, and even though the huge plane was tied down, it began flying. Ground handlers fi-nally got it under control, but not before it slammed into the hangar.

To reach the Naval Air Station Museum, watch for a blinker signal, two miles south of town. Turn east at the intersection, where a Douglas A4 is mounted by the road-side. (Also see Above the Coast section.)

North from Tillamook, the highway hugs the coast again through Garibaldi and Rockaway Beach. From Wheeler on, you may notice that even if the rest of the coast is a bit gloomy, this area is often blessed with clear-ing conditions.

Cannon Beach has a look all its own, which some-how manages to carry a feeling of an eastern seaport town where a California surf shop can be right at home. Oh, there are the inevitable parking problems, for those who want to park right in front of a restaurant. But this town has re-created itself in such a unique fashion, that most anything is forgivable. It's artsy without being high-brow, earthy without being camp. All in all, the kind of place you'll want to know better. Stick around, it wears well.

SEASIDE–ASTORIA

If Cannon Beach is a stroller's town, **Seaside** is a beach party—an all-out resort town, with everything from bumper cars to surfing. Check out the Million Dollar walk through shops and restaurants of every kind, with some of the best people-watching places on the Oregon coast. Great boardwalk, too. A fun place to overnight.

Tiny **Gearhart** makes the most of its uncrowded beauty, controlling development and retaining the origi-nal look of the Oregon coast. This is a place to come for solitude, a little laid-back golf, and a lot of beach walking. Nice condo rentals are available.

Nearing the end of US 101 in Oregon, there are still a few very special stops. Keep an eye out along the way for **Sunset Beach,** just under nine miles north of Gearheart. This is a lovely beach to drive on—and it was once declared a state highway to protect it from development. Great place for a picnic or a road break, and rarely crowded. On the way, at 3223 Sunset Beach Lane, is a nicely renovated building housing the Sunset Bakery, with a deli, and breads approaching the exotic.

TRAVELER'S NOTE: If you've been following our story of how the U.S. West Coast was shelled during World War II, Fort Stevens will be a definite stop. You'll also want to take in Fort Clatsop National Memorial, which recalls the Lewis and Clark period with a superb replica of the original fort. Allow a couple of hours for Fort Stevens and the wreck of the *Peter Iredale,* and a bit less at Fort Clatsop.

Choose Fort Clatsop if you're really short on time. Fort Worden at Port Townsend can serve as a stand-in for Fort Stevens. And if it's midafternoon or later, you might want to head on into Astoria, explore the Astoria Column plus the rest of Astoria, and return here in the morning. Otherwise, if you have plenty of daylight, press on.

CAMPING NOTE: You'll rarely find a better designed and maintained facility, with biking and riding and walking trails galore. So if you have some junior BMXers along, or someone still on training wheels, this is a good place to do a little pedaling. North of Santa Cruz, this is one of the most family-oriented parks you'll find.

And it is best done in the morning. Fewer people are about and the place has a quiet, almost reverent atmosphere.

If you're headed for Fort Stevens, exit on Ft. Stevens Highway, just before US 101 bends to the east. At the next opportunity, turn west on Oceanview Cemetery Road.

After a bend to the north and Delaura Beach Road, you'll find a small plaque placed there by the American Legion, to commemorate the shelling of Fort Stevens by the same I-25 submarine that shelled Ellwood Terminal north of Santa Barbara.

Under the redoubtable Lt. Commander Tagami, the sub surfaced on the night of June 21, 1942, and fired seventeen rounds without actually knowing the batteries of Fort Stevens were here.

Here, the plan was not only to frighten the public but to draw American patrol vessels into deep water where they could be sunk. But our guys hung tough. No return fire gave away Fort Stevens's position, and no ships were risked against a single, elusive target. And, as before, no damage was done. The I-25 returned to Japan.

Continue north and turn left on Peter Iredale Road, to view the ship's remains. A four-masted barque, the *Peter Iredale* ran aground in a storm on the night of October 15, 1906. And has been here ever since, decaying a little more each year, showing amazing resistance to wind and weather.

She's only a few rusted steel ribs now, easily reached at low tide. Children see her as an immense historic jungle gym. The rest of us see in her hulk a reminder of mankind's frailty—and our own mortality.

An exploration of Battery Russell, just up the road a bit, gives a fair impression of how these fortifications operated. But if you'd like to see a scale model of the whole thing, plus an emplacement that dates to the Civil War, return to Ridge Road and continue north to Fort Stevens's museum.

To visit Lewis and Clark's Fort Clatsop, you may either retrace your route or, if you are north in the museum area, drive down through **Warrenton.** The town has a few new buildings scattered here and there, but it all seems to fit right in. Mostly, the town looks just about as it would have in the 1940s. A nice, church-going town, and a good place to raise kids, cats, and dogs.

Either way, you will need to get yourself on US 101A, the Warrenton-Astoria Highway, and turn south into the Fort Clatsop parking area. The route is well-marked from most approaches.

Fort Clatsop is unlike anything we've been visiting along the coast. The other forts are designed to defend a coastline that we had acquired and made part of America, first against the British, then largely against all comers. By contrast, Fort Clatsop is more of a defended settlement that harks back to pioneer days in the Appalachians, across the Great Lakes area, and west.

Nestled in the trees, there is very little feeling of conquest here—more a sense of an exploration of nature and a (sometimes uneasy) partnership with surrounding Native Americans.

But more than anything else, Fort Clatsop has about it a sense of culmination and future challenge. Lewis and Clark's journey ended here. But having reached the Great Western Sea, the questions and problems that drove the expedition here remained unresolved.

So if Fort Clatsop is a physical celebration of a journey ended, it also conveys a sense of incompletion, something Meriwether Lewis carried with him to his death years later on the Natchez Trace.

From Fort Clatsop, it's easiest to reach Astoria by returning to US 101 and crossing Young's Bay on the causeway. And as you reach the lift-bridge section—with counterweights of hundreds of tons of concrete suspended above your head—be sure not to think about all that falling on your car.

Astoria is the oldest settlement west of the Rockies, and perfectly situated for its character, which defines much of what Oregon is about. A service town supplying the surrounding area, Astoria has managed to avoid the kind of recession that struck the rest of the coast with the decline in fisheries and timber. And there is a quality of life here reflecting the town's stability. It probably didn't hurt that the town is named for John Jacob Astor, a fairly classy guy, as traders go.

NAVIGATOR'S NOTE: When entering Astoria, either from US 101 or along the waterfront from Fort Clatsop, follow US 30, *not* US 101, which will only hustle you up onto the bridge—from which there is no exit—and prematurely into Washington.

Instead continue into town, for there are really some wonderful things to experience here. Remember Eureka? Astoria is the same sort of surprise. And like the good folks in Humboldt County, people here in Astoria are happy in being just a little off the wall.

For some quick highlights, and a trip up to the Astoria Column, turn right on 8th Street and begin following signs for the column. Not far up, you'll begin seeing scads of magnificent Victorians, including the remarkable Flavel House, dating from 1885, and now a museum, and the Rosebriar Hotel at 636 14th Street, now a charming B&B, the original structure was a convent.

Once on Coxcomb Drive, you'll be climbing through a rolling wooded area, with occasional views opening up behind. And by now, you're probably thinking something like, *Right. Another vertical monument. What's the fuss?* And that's good, because you'll be totally unprepared for what you find on Coxcomb Hill.

For the one-hundred-twenty-five-foot Astoria Column is part tower, part beacon, part monument, part petroglyph, and virtually indescribable.

The job of any monument is to impress past values on a fleeting present. When a monument combines that with a personal vision, we are witness to a mystery. That's what the Astoria Column is.

Travelers come expecting another ho-hum thumb in the sky, and leave both impressed and renewed in their own purpose. Where most monuments are dedicated to some person or event, the Astoria Column remarks on the flow of human consciousness leading to distant events in the American Far West. It's quite a journey.

The view of Astoria-Warrenton, both bridges, and the Columbia River is awesome from here. And if you have highly active children along, you'll be happy to know there are one hundred sixty-four steps to the top of the column.

Stop by the trippy little information booth, where classical music plays on a tiny loudspeaker. There, you can buy little balsa gliders to sail off the top of the column. Seventy cents apiece, or five for three dollars—the place is a hoot! Right down to the water dish placed conveniently by the door in case you have Fido along.

Returning to Marine Drive (Leif Erickson Drive farther east) you'll find plenty of waterfront lodgings. Most are only a few minutes from the Columbia River Maritime Museum at 1792 Marine Drive.

You could drive there, of course. But it's a whole lot more fun to take the Riverfront Trolley, *Old 300,* to your destination. Even if you don't visit the museum, the trolley ride is a kick. At the end of the run, passengers help out by reversing the seats for the return trip.

The trolley is a wonderful addition to the waterfront and seems never to have a shortage of riders. For those who find the trolley a lightweight, there's Desdemona's and Annie's Tavern Dancers back up the street. Just a little reminder that the old waterfront ain't dead yet.

Departing Astoria, pick up US 101 again as it coils up onto the bridge to Washington.

When crossing the Astoria-Megler Bridge, which was a pretty big thing around here when it opened in 1966—and the longest continuous truss-span bridge in the world—take it a little easy. The winds here really enjoy tossing RVs around.

WASHINGTON

One look at a state map shows that there is just an awful lot of water up here. Which is why so many travelers from arid Southern California head this way every year.

It is cool and damp and rainy here, and not crowded, nor likely to slide into the ocean—although some parts blow themselves up from time to time.

Which is why so many Washingtonians are not all that glad to see people from California. Because it's not only cool here, it is now cool to *be* here. And Southern Californians understand cool. They make a beeline for where cool is, invited or not.

Washington wasn't always that way. Lewis and Clark had a hell of a time getting here, and once they arrived, had no clear idea about what to do with the place. Lumbering interests and fisheries set up shop early; the rest took a little longer.

The biggest deal to come along was probably Grand Coulee Dam, ready to provide power to the entire Northwest, and certainly to Boeing Aircraft, as America staggered out of the Great Depression and into World War II.

Still, like most northern-tier states, Washington was pretty far from the action. If California was isolated until the 1950s, Washington was more so.

Yet the state has surged forward to become a leader. When the Space Needle was first constructed, other cities had a good chuckle. Soon the laughers all wanted bigger ones, Freudian implications and all.

Washington's fortunes really changed with the boom in technology, as Boeing grabbed the lead in construction of long-range jets, and Silicon Valley overflowed into the Pacific Northwest. For the first time, Seattle didn't need to be near the rest of the country, it was near itself. That was clearly enough, and with the possible exception of seasonal ennui among its ballclubs, still is.

SOUTHERN COAST

On reaching the shore in Washington, turn left to follow US 101, and notice the first Tsunami Evacuation Route signs. This state takes the big-wave threat very seriously, if only because there is evidence that a tsunami once came ashore here and traveled nearly two hundred miles inland.

And because the beaches are so often cliffbound, people in Washington take their tide-tables seriously, too. It's all too easy to be caught in a cove by a fast-rising tide, with no way up, or out. A tide table can be picked up free just about everywhere—don't go to the beach without it.

CHINOOK–SOUTH BEND

As you drive northwest along the coast toward Chinook, you'll be leaving the softer, more amiable landforms and weather of the Columbia River. All along the coasts of Oregon and Washington, the river-mouth areas have a gentler disposition, with fog and low clouds clearing here much earlier than along the bluffs and crags above the sea.

And as you approach the forests of Olympia National Park, you can figure on some rain (that's why they call them rain forests). To say nothing of place names like Storm King and Hurricane Ridge . . .

Some Washingtonians take the view that since moss doesn't grow in a desert, rain is the price for all this beauty. Others are more tourist-oriented. *It doesn't rain all that much here,* some will say, *we just like to keep our skies clean, so we wash them a lot.*

But it's hard to find a town that doesn't have a rain shop, with all kinds of slickers and other gear to keep you dry—especially when the winds come up and the rain goes horizontal.

Like the folks in Oregon, Washingtonians are inveterate storm watchers. When winter-season travelers are huddled in their vehicles, whole rows of yellow-slickered, gum-booted watchers are out along the shore watching the Mighty Pacific do its stuff. If you happen on a good storm, suit up and join them. It's actually a lot of fun.

Just past the tunnel, a left turn will take you into Fort Columbia. A drive-through only takes a few minutes, and it will be interesting to see what you make of this miniature post. It has much of the same 1900–1930 style of the Presidio in San Francisco, and Fort Worden far to the north. But this post is so removed physically from everything around it and so compressed, in order to fit on this rock, that the place achieves a feeling of intimacy. One can almost hear a small military band playing for dances—the smiles, the subdued gaiety.

You'll also see a definite change in the character of the towns along the route, as we drive farther north. **Chinook** looks like it's in for the long pull, with shops more attuned to daily business with locals. The town is also an unlikely place for an incredible restaurant. But the Sanctuary on US 101 at Hazel Street serves dinners Wednesdays through Sundays that are out of this world. If you are staying either in Astoria or Long Beach, it's worth the trip.

Just ten miles beyond Chinook is a turn to the Long Beach peninsula, and a side-trip you will not want to miss. Indeed, the Long Beach area is well worth an overnight stay, with plenty of time for browsing.

Ilwaco is on the way, with an interesting Heritage Museum. But no more so than Bubba's, a great Italian dive at 115 S. Pacific Highway where you'll encounter good food and the drill sergeant of pizzas.

If you have plenty of time and the weather is perfect, the drive down to Fort Canby State Park is very nice. However—and this is a judgment call—the time is better spent in **Long Beach,** where you will find yourself drawn into the West Coast's perpetual county fair.

Seaview is the gateway to it all, and there's just about everything here that you can imagine, ready to hook you in off the street and sell you a good time, some salt-water taffy, or a trifle you'd never show your mother. At the same time, Seaview and Long Beach are host to some of the finest small inns and restaurants you'll find anywhere. And as elsewhere, the B&Bs here all serve to perpetuate some bit of history.

One of these is The Lion's Paw Inn, surrounded by an ever-expanding flower garden, and screened by trees to bring a sense of quietude to guests.

Unpretentious and beautifully maintained, this home was by turns one of the nicest of the early houses built in the area, a brothel, and the region's first hospital. If you visit, it will be a source of some amazement that a single physician-surgeon and one nurse could haul a post-operative patient to the second floor by themselves.

Present owners of The Lion's Paw, and hosts extraordinaire, have done much restoration work and created a homey place in the process, contrasting dark woods with light-gathering windows. Back in its bordello days, it never looked like this.

Before its present incarnation, the house was boarded up for some time, and some said there were ghostly presences. But a new owner was totally unprepared for what she found on a first inspection tour. As she climbed the stair, she became aware of a pungent musky smell that increased as she reached the upstairs hallway.

Now, the woman knew the place had been a brothel, and that the girls' rooms were off this hall. But such an odor, after all these years? At last, she opened one of the doors—to find mushrooms everywhere, growing up through the carpet.

The Lion's Paw is now far more sedate, and certainly drier. Furnished with both taste and whimsy—and offering superb breakfasts—the rates here begin at a moderate $80. At 3310 Pacific Highway South, as you enter Seaview. (800-553-2320)

On into Long Beach, probably the first thing to head for is the sand. You'll see parking along the street. But what the hell, if it's low tide, you can just drive on out, go as far as you want, and set up housekeeping.

That's something locals prize here: on kite-flying day, there may be five thousand kites in the air and at least twice that number on the other end of the strings. Yet you can trundle up the peninsula and be completely alone.

In town, bumper cars (and boats) compete with book vendors. And it's all quite wonderful. But there's a place—like no other on this planet—where you can have a terrific time for nothing. And that would be Marsh's Free Museum.

The place has been around since 1921, and some of the folks there are not much newer—though if you walk in with a mauve left-handed whipsnitch, someone at Marsh's will find the matching piece.

But we might as well start with Jake the Alligator Man. Half pygmy, half reptile. Is he real? Did he crawl from some primordial swamp? Or did he hitchhike here? All questions are of equal merit at Marsh's.

That's only a beginning. The place has seashells everywhere, plus the shell of a six-hundred-pound Brazilian turtle. There are peep shows, a 1940 Wendell Wilkie for President poster, a 10¢ Kiss Tester, plus a freeze-dried cat named Morris. And you get a free shell just for walking in. They give away about 150,000 shells a year. Maybe someone will top Marsh's act some day. But after seeing the place, you'll wonder how.

On up the peninsula there are more wonders, a bit of wilderness, and Oysterville. The harvesters here took enough oysters to make this the richest town around, with more gold coin per capita than anyplace but San Francisco. But the oyster beds were farmed out, Oysterville's railroad disappeared, and another town stole the county seat.

Yet for all this carnival atmosphere, Long Beach never seems to wear thin. People keep coming back. The world's ugliest mermaid is here to greet them, and on it goes.

Farther north on US 101, **South Bend** proclaims itself oyster capital of the world, which it may well be. We pretty much need to take their word for it. The town is also working adaptive reuse for existing structures, and it's difficult. But this *is* the county seat at least—because South Bend is the town that swiped it from Oysterville.

Having driven this far, by now you know Washington's dirty little secret—caffeine is the drug of choice up here. There are espresso bars and barns and boxes, espresso drive-thrus, and the stuff is even sold in lieu of popcorn in local movie theaters that would otherwise be shuttered and dark.

So as you drive through this beautiful state, along first-class highways, be aware that a large number of the cars you meet up with will be driven by people who are totally wired.

Olympic Peninsula

Of the three Pacific Coast states, Washington undoubtedly has the finest highways. But the weather hereabouts is tough on surfaces, and one result of Washingtonians' pride in their roads is that they are always out there fixing them.

Delays with single-file traffic and Follow Me vehicles are a fact of life here. Just knowing that ahead of time will make these little stops less frustrating. So if you are stopped and see no traffic headed in your direction, with few vehicles behind you, it could be awhile. So relax. Turn off the engine. And since it's a good bet you'll be deep in a forest somewhere, enjoy being exactly where you are. Have an apple.

ABERDEEN–LAKE QUINAULT

Again, on a flat, river plain, **Aberdeen** has the low look of a city planned to have weather blow right on over it. Which is what some unfortunate sailors should have done. For their union was headed by one of the all-time bad guys, Billy Gohl. Up until the early 1920s, the sailors would give their money to Billy to keep for them. When they came back to claim it, typically a little boozy, Billy would tell them to go right on over to the safe and open it, and when they did, Billy would sap them from behind and drop the bodies through a trapdoor right into the river.

For some years, these bodies went out to sea unnoticed

or turned up as floaters somewhere in the bay. Well, Billy was finally nailed for his grisly work, went to prison, and died in a mental ward—but not before he'd killed between two hundred and two hundred fifty unsuspecting sailors. Downriver is where it all happened.

Following US 101 north across the Chehalis River and into town, you'll discover a public transit terminal rendered so delightful that it's hard to imagine there's no train coming. Something whimsical from Steven Spielberg, maybe? But no, this is all part of a bus system of which the Grays Harbor area is rightfully proud. Climb on a bus in Grayland, to the south, and ride all the way to Quinault—close to seventy-five miles—for a quarter.

Aberdeen's Historic Seaport is home to the *Lady Washington,* a lovely one-hundred-seventy-ton replica of a brig first launched in Massachusetts in 1750. This 1989 version is a floating classroom and a Tall Ship ambassador for the state of Washington, appearing also in *Star Trek Generations.* She is a living reminder that our history is not so confluent as we like to believe.

Rituals and offerings were recently performed aboard the vessel, intending to heal old wounds inflicted by the original ship and captain on the Haida (Children of Eagle and Raven), native inhabitants of the Queen Charlotte Islands. The healing may take some time, yet it is underway thanks to the ship's company and *Lady Washington.*

If you're into rugged individualism, stop in **Hoquiam** for a look at Hoquiam's Castle at 515 Chenault Street, a Victorian home to one of two timber-baron brothers. It's an eye-popper and on the National Register. The Lytle House, home to the other brother, is now an exceptional B&B, next door. Watch for Chenault three blocks after US 101 returns to two-way traffic.

Theater buffs will enjoy the original woodsy-baroque interior of the 7th Street Theater, now completely restored.

As you depart Hoquiam, you notice that US 101 takes an interesting squiggle on the map. Instead of running on west and along the coast as WA 109 does for some distance, the highway remains inland. A second look will tell you why. The Quinault Nation has been able to hang tough all these years, without allowing a through highway or development to occur along the coastal portion of their reservation. And some heavy hitters have been out here from Washington, D.C., too. No dice. If it is ever done, it must be on the Quinaults' terms. Meanwhile we're on our way to beautiful Lake Quinault, which we might otherwise have missed.

Along the highway, from Hoquiam north, you'll see that the sections of forest that have been taken have placards indicating when the section was clear-cut and when new growth was begun. And for sections clear-cut back in the 1930s, the new growth looks quite good.

Of course, it took sixty years or so. And of greater interest is the relentless order in which the new plantings occur—all the same height, spaced symmetrically. It's green, and it will certainly yield lumber, which is the purpose here. Still, it looks a lot more like a factory than a forest.

North of tiny **Humptulips**—which means *hard to pole* in the language of the Quinault tribe, and refers to difficulty in poling wood canoes against the river's current—the road takes on a new character, running nearly straight up to Quinault. Here, the trees are so tall and the highway so narrow by comparison, that the drive almost feels like the long passage down the nave of an evergreen cathedral—truly breathtaking. You may want to slow for a bit through this stretch, it passes quickly. And it may not be this way for long. The government is cutting farther back from the road.

This is also an area once known by lumbermen as the Promised Land. The virgin growth of trees here was so thick, and the trees themselves so big—only one is left to remind us of what giants they were—that it was almost impossible to fell a tree here.

But ways were found, of course, and from this small area, uncounted *billions* of board feet of lumber were harvested. We shall never see anything like it again.

When a glacier covering all this land packed it up and moved back up north, **Lake Quinault** was left as a memento and it is truly a gorgeous place.

At Quinault, there's a turnoff for Lake Quinault Lodge on the south shore. Just a bit farther, at Amanda Park, you'll find the turnoff for Lake Quinault Resort. If you'll be staying over—and that's a really good idea—a room at either will do the trick. Yet they are as different as can be.

Lake Quinault Lodge, done in a parklands style, is a perfect introduction to the rain forests of the Olympic Peninsula. The lodge site dates from the mid-1800s. Dark and woodsy, it is a reminder of a time when there seemed to be time—to enjoy a bit of elegant conversation, read a book in the great room, take tea on the lawn, enjoy an un-hurried dinner by candlelight.

Only a part of an earlier lodge, which burned in 1924, remains. Today's main structure was designed by an archi-tectural firm known for work on Old Faithful Inn at Yel-lowstone National Park, so the parklands look is no accident. And the same work patterns followed at the Del in San Diego served well here. With bonfires for round-the-clock labor, the main lodge went up in a record fifty-three days, opening on August 18, 1924.

But the highlight of lodge history was undoubtedly a visit by President Franklin D. Roosevelt. In the late 1800s, an Olympic Forest Reserve of over two million acres had been authorized by Grover Cleveland, earning him threats of impeachment. Later, when Teddy Roo-sevelt established Mount Olympus National Monument, the mining and timber interests went absolutely ballistic. Woodrow Wilson later cut the acreage by half, outraging conservationists, and the dispute over preservation still rages in many quarters today.

By the 1930s, lumbering interests agreed that it would be fine to have a park, but a *little* one. Conservationists wanted most of the peninsula preserved for future gener-ations and as a total ecological system that could teach us, as our own knowledge grew, how such systems work to nurture mankind.

As the issue fueled open political warfare, FDR came west in 1937 to see what could be done, and stayed at Lake Quinault Lodge, virtually guaranteeing its recogni-tion as a first-class inn. The dining room still carries his name. Today, after many changes over the years, Lake Quinault Lodge has largely been restored. And it is a gem!

Guest rooms here echo the fine touches of the lobby. Rates for rooms and suites range from under $70 to $280, depending on season and location. (360-288-2900)

And where else could you while away a few hours pitching turn-of-the-century horseshoes or playing croquet? Even if you only have time for a meal, be sure to include a walk down to the gazebo on the lakeshore, and a look back up at the lodge. Peaceful, elegant, and a perfect part of these surroundings.

On the north side of the lake is an entirely different lodging experience. Lake Quinault was literally rebuilt from the ashes of a fire caused by some meth-cookers who had rented one of the units. In the process, the place has taken on some of the gentle identity of its new owners. In a lovely setting fetching down to the crystal-clear lake, this intimate resort has the forest and its solitude for a backdrop, with trailheads close at hand.

Rates for beautifully appointed rooms, suites, and kitchenettes range from $50 to $129, depending on season. (360-288-2362)

But the real character of this place takes a while to come through. Be sure to ask either of the owners about the arbor beams out front, and the decking below your feet. The answers will surprise and delight you.

AMANDA PARK–FORKS

Although Lake Quinault is in a rain forest, the Hoh Valley and its rain forest really get the action: one hundred fifty inches or more—that's fourteen feet of the wet stuff—per year. And that's where we're headed, with a stop along the way at **Kalaloch.** Here you'll find Kalaloch Lodge—which, if you were unable to find accommodations at Lake Quinault—is marvelous in itself. Perched (almost precariously) on a bluff above the sea, this old-timer may be the quintessential oceanfront lodge, with weathered shake siding and the classic look of a Pacific Northwest resort. No beach umbrellas around here. Instead, everyone is out on nature walks, or watching the peregrine falcons, whales, and dolphins that populate the National Marine Sanctuary, of which Kalaloch Lodge is a part. The restaurant is superb, and there's a lounge and coffee shop as well. Accommodations range from attractive rooms in the main lodge to very nice cabins, with rates from $50 to $211, depending on season. (360-962-2271)

Just a half mile farther on is the Kalaloch Campground—and it's super! A little more rustic than some of the top Oregon campgrounds, but the setting here is unmatched. Even if you're not a camper or are planning to overnight at the lodge, spend a little time here if possible. And if it's even remotely close to mealtime, dodge on down to the general store next door to the lodge and pick up whatever you need.

About seven miles farther on is Ruby Beach. Even in fog, this place can be magical. Just the romance will get you: couples huddled in blankets on bluffs overlooking the sea, other couples walking slowly along in lockstep, wrapped in a sleeping bag. But it's tough on writers traveling alone . . .

A few yards beyond Ruby Beach, US 101 turns inland for about ten miles along the Hoh River, and just north of Hoh-Oxbow Campground, you'll find the entrance to the Hoh Rain Forest. A visitor center is a little over fifteen miles farther on, and that will help you decide which trails to explore, given the time you have available. Because this is all so lush, so fairy-talelike that it's easy to become lost in the experience.

You'll also need to come up with the entry fee for the Olympic National Park (currently $10 and good for seven days). But the permit can be used again near Port Angeles for the mythic drive up to Hurricane Ridge.

You've probably realized by now that what began as a fun little drive along Southern California beaches has become something of an adventure. The promise was made by the road just north of San Francisco, in Mendocino County, and renewed again among the seastacks along Oregon's coast. But here on the Olympic Peninsula, Pacific Coast Highway makes good on all of it—primitive shoreline, wildlife of nearly every description, mountains, resorts among thousand-year-old trees, and moss growing everywhere but inside your hat.

This country and the people who have chosen to live here and nurture all that surrounds them is the peak adventure of all. The rain forests are the beginning—and if you are able to take in all you find here—it gets even better.

From the Hoh Rain Forest, US 101 will carry you to **Forks** (and they don't much care for silverware jokes up here), which is a good place to check road conditions ahead and pick up travel information at the Forks Chamber of Commerce Visitor Center across from the airport on what is actually the south side of the road.

To get a feeling of this region, visit the Timber Museum. Or, if you're short on daylight, look in on the Loggers' Memorial, just a few feet from the center. It's easy to choose a side of the ongoing debate over trees versus timber and forget the human toll involved in development of any resource.

One look at the size of the tackle used in lumbering makes clear the hellish forces involved. It's worth a moment to read the names of the men lost just in this one place. Whatever our views today, it is still an honor roll.

Forks is a dandy place to take a late breakfast or lunch and there are also several nice places in town to stay (See Food and Lodging) because this is a major jumping-off point for hunters and fishermen.

Just north of Forks, there is a choice-point. If you are a fisherman or a photographer who likes working more primitive images, drive over to LaPush, a Quileute Indian village, and First Beach, which attracts both kayakers and surfers. Rialto Beach, farther north, often offers better surfing. Second Beach to the south is more photogenic. LaPush is actually a corruption of the French, *La Bouche,* referring to the mouth of the Quileute River.

The Quileutes have a strong seafaring tradition. And to make that point abundantly clear, Quileute Tribe members put on a Paddle-to-Seattle challenge in their handmade canoes. Not content with that journey, they later made an eight-hundred-mile voyage to Bella Bella. If you've done any canoeing or kayaking, that story's got to make your shoulders hurt.

It's about twenty-four miles round-trip, or you may want to stay at the lodge in LaPush. Take WA 110 west, bend south at the fork, onto LaPush Road, and just keep going.

SAPPHO–LAKE CRESCENT

Continuing on north, US 101 winds through the Sol Duc Valley. At tiny **Sappho,** you'll have another choice, but this one is a must-do, if you are in an exploring frame of mind. Here, you can take WA 113 north, and WA 112 west to Neah Bay and out to Cape Flattery.

From **Clallam Bay** west, the road hugs the shore of the Strait of Juan de Fuca through dipsy-doddles and tight bends. So once again, vans and anything larger will be at some risk. That's before you factor in the logging trucks. Because some of those guys have been driving this road for *years,* they've got a schedule to meet—and trust me on this—you will not like being in the way.

Notice, too, that the farther west you drive, the more tightly knit the villages become. Even with a nod toward charter fishing and the like, there is a tribal feeling here that makes itself felt even passing by on the road.

At **Neah Bay,** you'll be in for a special treat, for the Makah Museum is internationally known for the nature of its collection and its well-designed displays. The Research Center there began some on-site digs in 1970 at the village of Ozette, which had suffered from a catastrophic mudslide, probably started by an earthquake.

From an archaeological viewpoint, this represents a major find of well-preserved Makah artifacts dating back at least five hundred years. By contrast, many of the common artifacts of tribal life, which were collected largely by Europeans, only date back to the time of their arrival in North America.

Makah society was a class society, rather than a clan society, and had three tiers. On the top were the whalers and oceangoing fishermen; in the middle were the folks who handled community business; at the bottom were slaves—members of other tribes unlucky enough to be caught out in the open.

The interesting thing about Makah society was that the ocean was divided into hunting and fishing plots, far more than the land, with the focus here on the sea as the great provider. The land played a supporting role, with the great cedar trees furnishing what was needed—from canoes to clothing—to continue the harvest.

For the traveler, the Makah Museum can in many ways

reveal more of what underlies Pacific Northwest culture than can be found elsewhere. The place is indeed a small wonder. (Call 360-645-2711 for hours; closed Monday and Tuesday in winter.)

Oregon claims one of its coastal bulges is the westernmost point in the lower forty-eight states. So **Cape Flattery** misses the mark a bit from a geographic point of view. But when you go there, stand out on the point and look around—it sure as hell feels like this is the end of the line. You could get religion out here, and it's not surprising that Native Americans found this place holy. To reach the cape—and it's worth the seven-mile journey—continue west from the museum, through the curve, and to the Makah Tribal Center. The road shortly becomes gravel; continue on for four miles. At the sign for Cape Trail, swing left and park. Follow the left fork at the trailhead. If you are in fair condition, the trail isn't too difficult.

Whether you choose the side trip to Neah Bay or not, continue east from Sappho on US 101 (rather than WA 112) for beautiful **Lake Crescent,** a one-thousand-foot-deep glacial trough, nearly nine miles long. The drive along the south shore is spectacular and Lake Crescent Lodge is not to be missed.

Along the south-shore drive, you'll find a lovely picnic area at La Poel; the lodge will turn up about four miles later. Several cottages were added to the main lodge for FDR's visit in 1937, and famed Marymere Falls, dropping threadlike over ninety feet, is just a short—and fairly easy—walk away.

About eight miles east of Lake Crescent, just across the Elwha River, US 101 makes an abrupt left turn and takes on a commercial look. Instead, you may continue on east past that intersection as the road winds through the foothills and makes its way more pleasantly down to the Strait.

PORT ANGELES–PORT TOWNSEND

The entry into **Port Angeles** couldn't be nicer. After dozens of pretty towns turned tacky by strip development, Port Angeles looks like the kind of place you'd want to live in. As you roll down the hill toward the harbor, the courthouse, along with well-kept homes and businesses, speak for this small city and the people who keep it so well.

Port Angeles also has a couple of very good things going. It is on the edge of a rain shadow extending from the Olympic Mountains and enjoys very nice weather. The city is also a terminal for ferries to Victoria, British Columbia, and because this part of Washington depends so much on ferries, it is all a first-class operation.

On the waterfront, at 121 E. Railroad Avenue, you'll find a very helpful visitor center with maps and information.

One side trip not to miss while in the Port Angeles area is the drive up (and I mean *up*) Race Street and the highway beyond to **Hurricane Ridge.** Vans and smaller RVs will be able to negotiate this highway quite well, and the views are spectacular.

This is a drive best done in the morning—unless you are a stargazer in search of places with clear air and no city lights—*and* with at least three-quarters of a tank of fuel. Any vehicle will become a gas-guzzler on a grade like this, and it's a lot nicer not to have that old sinking sensation as the gas gauge falls before your eyes.

Still, for the first twenty minutes of this drive, you may be wondering if a pizza might not have been a better investment. Then you'll come around the first big bend—with the mountains stretching out to the east—and you'll know! Further, you'll be clearer than ever about what drew President Roosevelt west to settle the matter of these lands.

Hurricane Ridge is filled with trailheads and wonderful picnic places, so enjoy. And for blanket-cuddling romantics, it's hard to beat sunset-watching from Hurricane Hill Trail, just past the lodge.

One last item for driver-gawkers (as many of us admittedly are): the roadway here is wide and easy. However, there is not a single guardrail anywhere. If you drift too far over, the term *sheer drop* takes on a whole new meaning.

Now, before leaving the shadow of the Olympic Mountains and forests, some of which have yet to be fully explored, the sasquatch deserves mention. This is not the bigfoot of media fame, however. That sorry business depends only on people who say they saw something, and a medium that doesn't much care what it was so long as they talk about it on camera.

No, this is about sightings from reliable witnesses, and casts of footprints meeting academic standards, little of which is ever reported because it has no sizzle. Yet these may suggest that large, hairy bipeds with size twenty-four feet still roam this region, and have for as long as Native Americans have been here. Because the names for sasquatch are as old as tribal memory. And early peoples were concrete in their thinking—survival required it. They typically had words only for something that existed.

Meanwhile, anthropologists and others continue to sift through a growing body of physical evidence. But what's really needed is a first-class sighting by an impartial observer, someone not from the Olympic region, a traveler perhaps.

The trouble is sasquatch is almost never seen by outsiders. Wait—what's that, over there on the right, by the treeline . . . ?

Heading east on US 101, you'll be driving right into the epicenter of Washington's Weather Wars. While Port Angeles draws about twenty-four inches of rain per year, **Sequim** (*Skwim*) has only about sixteen inches. The town even bills itself as Sunny Sequim, with three hundred five days of clear weather per year.

How sunny is that? Well, sunny enough that a tiny version of the prickly pear cactus (about as big as your thumb) grows here. Sequim also claims that rainfall increases by one inch per mile as you drive east. Port Townsend disputes that, and points out that on many of their sunny days, Sequim is socked in. And so it goes.

But Sequim doesn't even let itself off lightly. In 1995 a Sunshine Ordinance was adopted, requiring anyone who causes bad weather to apologize publicly for their actions. The weather even leaks over into the names of local businesses. One is the Rainshadow Greenhouse, at 205 W. Washington, where you might want to stop in to see some truly marvelous topiary—not just cleverly trimmed plants, but living sculpture of the most charming and whimsical sort.

Nearing Sequim, take the River Road exit and you'll

find yourself back on old US 101. Entering town, there's a bit of strip-mall fever going on, but the downtown section is turning around. The 101 Diner, in the west end of town at 4th, is a nice bit of adaptive reuse, and the city planning department is itself housed in a renovated structure, right across from the Museum & Art Center, at 175 W. Cedar.

Sequim is also home to John Wayne Marina, named for its benefactor, the Duke, who had some pretty rascally times up this way aboard his converted World War II minesweeper, the *Wild Goose.*

If you've never driven—or walked—through a wild-animal park, there's a good one near here. Olympic Game Farm is a safe haven for members of several endangered species and a most friendly place. Follow the signs to 383 Ward Road, north of town.

East of town there's a little freeway nuisance, but it's over quickly and the drive continues through rolling woodlands.

Just past Gardiner, however, US 101 swings south. Instead, we'll curve around Discovery Bay for about twelve miles on WA 20, heading for **Port Townsend**—the northernmost point on our tour and a true highlight of this journey. Travelers who come here, whether from Seattle or Hong Kong, acknowledge that this town, far more than most, finds a soft spot in their hearts.

Approaching Port Townsend along the shoreline, you'll notice the large number of wooden boats—recall that their seams don't open up in colder water. The large number of Woodies here is also because Port Townsend is home to the Wooden Boat Foundation, which promotes traditional maritime skills and is known worldwide for their boatbuilding and sailing classes.

The heart of any experience of Port Townsend begins at the east end of town, with a display of vintage railroad cars, locomotives, and an outstanding display of sculpture. The immediate impression is that this is a pretty classy place, and it is.

With a lively nightlife and Centrum for the Arts, which attracts artists in every medium, the cultural side of Port Townsend is self-renewing. Indeed, the word *picturesque* is an apt term for this place. In relishing its heritage, and capitalizing on it, the entire town has become a picture postcard.

A stop at the visitor information center will be helpful. Look for it on a tiny triangle of land to your right between Benedict and Decatur. Be sure to pick up a map. And it's a very good idea, especially in summer, to drive back two blocks to the Park & Ride, and take the free shuttle downtown. Limited public parking is also available near the Quincy Street dock—which happens to be the prime location for *Snow Falling on Cedars*—but Park & Ride is a better deal.

As each block of the central district opens up new surprises, it's hard to realize what a tough time this town really had. For a large part of its life, Port Townsend was itself a soiled dove. Back in the mid-1800s, residents here were absolutely certain that it would be the state's grandest city, largest port, and the biggest enchilada around.

Money poured in—hence, the magnificent Victorian homes, store buildings and hotels. For Port Townsend not only had a terrific spot on the Strait, it would soon have the Pacific Northwest's largest railhead as well. The perfect combination. In typical Washingtonese, residents claimed that Port Townsend was as big as New York—except the town wasn't finished yet. Heady stuff.

Except, in 1890, the Union Pacific Railroad decided that the tracks were not coming here after all. Rather, the railhead would be in a sleepy little town called Seattle. At Port Townsend, the Victorian roof fell in.

The town stumbled along as high-class homes became lower-class bordellos. The army established Fort Worden in 1902, and there were flirtations with paper pulp, but business never seemed to get much better. Except for the folks up on the hill, of course, who always do all right in any town.

And so it went. Until the 1960s and early '70s, when semi-hippies began buying or leasing houses and renting rooms to their friends. Mind you, elegant Victorian homes were by then selling for $3,000–$10,000.

Soon after came the artists. Remember the good deals they found in Laguna and Venice and Sausalito? It was repeated here as they also set up shop in these grossly undervalued properties. B&Bs began handling weekenders, shopkeepers filled in the downtown area. *Et voilà:* Port Townsend, Historic Victorian Seaport!

And it is a marvel. Stroll—but don't try to drive—the main section of town to your heart's content. Port Townsend is browser-friendly. But if you want to get a true sense of the place, along with its quaint, haughty, and naughty stories, the best thing to do is call Port Townsend Sidewalk Tours.

The owners are hip history hounds and you'll love every minute of their one-hour tours. Even better, they can meet you on short notice. So give them a call (360-385-1967) when you hit town, catch a bite to eat, and you're on your way.

Or if you are a do-it-yourselfer, they'll tell you where to pick up a copy of their self-guiding book on classic Victorian homes. Either way, don't miss the opportunity to go beyond the storefronts and lace curtains, and into the life of a town that once flourished—and almost died—here.

Typical of the adaptive struggle of the town is the Bishop Victorian Hotel. Built by an English seaman who scored early in Port Townsend's history and was certain more warehouse space would be needed, the building was completed in practically the same breath as Union Pacific's dream-smashing announcement.

Since then the structure has had owners as diverse as Owl Cigars and the U.S. Navy. Under present ownership, however, the structure has surpassed all prior hopes and is, or soon will be, a four-star inn. Design themes in the parlorlike lobby are those of William Morris, a Victorian-era designer known for his work on transatlantic liners like the *Titanic* and *Olympia*.

The hotel is done with impeccable taste, with fireplace rooms, many having tubs as well as showers, and all the amenities. Suites are from $69 to $169. Admirably hosted, the Bishop Victorian, at 714 Washington Street, offers a perfect sense of time and place. (360-385-6122)

Manresa Castle, now operated largely as a B&B, (look for its golden dome near the hospital on Sheridan) has a checkered history as well. Built by the city's first mayor, who happened to be Prussian and very castle-oriented, it was a financial statement with thirty rooms. Some twenty years later it became a vacation home for nuns from Seattle, and then a college for Jesuit priests. The Old Consulate Inn and Palace Hotel have similar histories—every place in town has its own story to tell.

Now, on to Fort Worden, certainly the most striking of all the posts we've visited! Return east on Washington Street and turn right on Walker Street. At Jefferson, you'll be on a level with the courthouse, and it's worth a cruise around the block. Continue on Walker as it angles right and becomes Cherry Street, which will take you to the gates of Fort Worden State Park.

An Officer and a Gentleman was filmed here (my gosh, has it really been nearly twenty years?), and as you drive around the parade ground and past the barracks, scenes may begin to roll again in your mind.

Over there was where the recruits first formed up; here was where Richard Gere ate mud rather than quit, over there . . . and so on. The film has held up exceptionally well over the years and remains one of the perennial favorites at video shops. After your visit, you'll love it all over again.

Before leaving this area, also notice the building that now houses the little theater. Brochures note that it was originally a barn for mules. Nope, just the army pulling the taxpayer's leg again. The building was actually built to house observation balloons.

But the army's experience in the balloon business was pretty well confined to the Civil War and the easier climate of the Southeast—which prepared no one for weather in the Northwest. Put a balloon up any distance here and you can bet that it'll end up in Iowa.

So the army disposed of the balloons, renamed the building "Mule Barn," and that became its official standing in history.

If you enjoyed clambering over the emplacements at Fort Stevens, these are even moodier and more mysterious. For a look around, drive out to the Point Wilson Lighthouse first, then head back, turn right at the first parking lot and right again to the end. Just a short walk from there.

As with Fort Stevens, the batteries here used disappearing naval rifles. Mounted in deep circular emplacements, these guns were lifted on their mounts, fired, and lowered again to be reloaded. The advantage was that they were visible only for a few seconds and would be hard to spot.

But it didn't work out that way. Smoke and muzzle blast from a big gun is visible for miles. What's worse, the Fort Worden batteries were heavily outgunned by battle-ships of the day. To the last man, soldiers stationed at Fort Worden knew that the Japanese—or any other fleet—could simply stand offshore, out of range, and this entire installation would be shot to pieces.

Imagine the courage it took to remain at your post early in World War II with such knowledge—and the first line of defense lying on the bottom at Pearl Harbor. You might want to bear some of that in mind as you explore these aging concrete ramparts we were lucky not to have to defend.

PORT LUDLOW–QUILCENE

Departing Port Townsend on WA 20, you can connect with US 101 southbound immediately, or spend a little more time on this lovely sub-peninsula.

And I'm not above bribing you a little. By taking the drive to **Port Ludlow** (see Lodging), you'll also have a shot at Ferino's, one of the area's most prolific pizza places. These guys *really* turn out the pies.

To do the Scenic Pizza route, bend left on WA 19, con-tinue to Ness' Corner Road and turn left again. Ferino's will come up on your right after a bit.

Continue east through a couple of right bends and

you'll be driving on an uncrowded two-lane along the shore. Down from Port Ludlow, loop around through South Point and Dabob to pick up southbound US 101. That will take you through **Quilcene,** which is the world's largest oyster hatchery. You could stop and watch, but oyster hatching occurs at a pretty slow pace.

BRINNON–OLYMPIA

The drive along this shoreline can be thought-provoking as well as beautiful. It is not well-developed along here. If you are a shellfish fan, you may be wondering how it is that you live where you do and not *here.*

A lot of current residents in **Brinnon** felt that way, and it's now largely a retirement community—which also happened to be getting a raw deal from the state not long ago. Well, you don't mess with gray around here. No, sir. Brinnon voted to secede from Washington, through-traffic on US 101 was shut down, and the state suddenly decided to listen. Go gray!

Just north of Potlatch State Park, you'll notice a WPA-style building. What's more, it's a power plant—not usually given to esthetic design. But this one is a beauty.

If you live near the coast and buy your Christmas tree in a local market, it's a good bet it came from **Shelton.** This area ships about three million each season. Just south of here, US 101 becomes a freeway that will carry you to Olympia or Seattle.

As cities and state capitals go, **Olympia** is lovely. Open, green, with enough room to swing your arms. This city is also where we'll be parting company. The US 101 portion of Pacific Coast Highway ends here, as does our journey together.

It has been my pleasure to go along with you on this tour of Pacific Coast Highway—we did have a time or two back there, didn't we?—and I wish you many happy journeys to come.

With peace and love.

ALTERNATE ROUTES

When you recognize that some parts of California are riding tectonic plates that are galloping west and north at rates of up to a foot per year, it will not be surprising that highways on the sea-rim are sometimes blocked by landslides. And when that happens it can take months, or years, to repair.

Rerouting occurs most often on CA 1 south of Carmel, through Malibu, and in the north around Mendocino. So here is a mini-guide designed to make a detour both lively and interesting.

SOUTHERN CALIFORNIA

HOLLYWOOD-WOODLAND HILLS

If you are northbound and have driven into Los Angeles, only to find the Pacific Coast Highway closed in Malibu, you could end up on the freeway through **Hollywood.** Here, US 101 pretty much rushes to get out of town. Universal City is a possibility, but little else. And unless it's early in the day or later in the evening, US 101 here will probably be jammed.

So here's the plan. Jump off the freeway at the Sunset Boulevard exit and enjoy driving Sunset through a far more interesting part of Hollywood. Just stay on it all the way to Westwood Village and I-405, which you can join northbound for the San Fernando Valley. There you'll be able to pick up US 101 and rejoin the coast at Ventura.

Near the top of the grade on the west side of the freeway, you'll see the spectacular new Getty Museum, with its Disney-like busways. If you are in an art museum frame of mind, there are few experiences to equal the Getty. It really is a wow.

Cresting the hill, make your way into the second lane from the right. And do this fairly soon, because it can really stack up near the bottom, where you'll be transitioning to the Ventura Freeway (US 101) westbound, while the far right-hand lane will be shunted off toward Los Angeles.

Headed west now, you'll pass through seamless valley communities until you reach **Woodland Hills,** which was and is the end of the line for the metropolitan Los Angeles area. Comfortable, tree-lined residential streets flank the 101 freeway to the south, and an amazing development on the site of Jack Warner's former ranch helps redefine the notion of commercial development, with carefully integrated corporate offices, shopping plazas, and housing, all looking as though it is exactly right.

WESTLAKE VILLAGE–CAMARILLO

Part of the inspiration for Warner Center came from **Westlake Village,** which was developed by the same company that created Westwood Village, commercial godfather to what UCLA is today. If the Libertarians could vote for their favorite town, Westlake would be a top contender. For some years, Westlake Village had a Barbie doll look about it, but times change, and what we once thought to be cutting-edge plastic now looks . . . comfortable.

If Westlake is settled in its ways, **Thousand Oaks** is still on the trail of its identity. Once a stage stop on a dusty plain dotted by thousands of oak trees, the town represented tourism—an ancestor of all wild-animal parks, Lion Farm attracted visitors here from the

1930s—and apricot farmers. Not incorporated until 1964, the town is now working to free itself of an early burst of marginal development.

Newbury Park and **Camarillo** are both the benefactors and the victims of freeway development. Certainly their residential areas would not have developed without easy access to L.A. At the same time, when schools were integrated in Los Angeles, White Flight became the by-word here, and both communities were changed.

Newbury Park has since attracted a number of high-tech industries, keeping many of its former commuters home, and Camarillo, once the site of a sleepy state hospital, is now the happy parent of a new state university campus on the former hospital grounds. Things don't move quickly in ranch-bound Ventura County, but sometimes they move along fairly well.

A bit of history is also well-displayed in Newbury Park, at the Stagecoach Inn Museum, just south of US 101 off Ventu Park Road. What's impressive about this museum site is that it offers a glimpse into several other cultural periods, including Chumash and Californio.

CENTRAL CALIFORNIA

SOLVANG–ARROYO GRANDE

Above Santa Barbara, just off the route, but worth a look-see, is little **Solvang.** Pitching itself as the Danish Capital of America, this community can probably claim more tourists per capita than anyone.

Once you see the place, you'll understand why. If Walt Disney had ever decided to construct a Pastryland, it would look just like Solvang. And the pastries are wonderful. So is the shopping and browsing. Everything from antiques to wine. And for roadies into quaint architecture, the gawkfactor here is close to 100 percent.

Right next door, **Buellton** has never been a town to miss out on a good thing. Okay, so Denmark is taken. How about we do an Avenue of the Flags? But the main attraction here is Pea Soup Andersons, a California roadside tradition for over seventy-five years. Everyone stopped for pea soup—and good food of every sort, plus friendly, home-town service from apple-scrubbed youngsters—and a chance to be in a place that is as traditional as anything to be found along the coast. And they still do. Plan a bite to eat here, no matter what time of day it is. At 376 Avenue of the Flags—though you won't need an address to find it.

King of the hill in the agricultural part of Santa Barbara County, **Santa Maria** houses well over half the valley's residents. And the town reflects a closeness to planting and harvest. There's a wide-open feeling to the highway as it rolls over low hills and flatlands, showing an enormous increase in acreage supporting new vineyards. With the exception of industrial pockets in the northern and southern parts of the state, wine is on its way to becoming California's chief industry. We could do worse—and have.

Arroyo Grande has a dual personality, part agricultural, part let's-go-to-the-beach. And it's a pleasant mix. Back in the 1930s, though, this entire area was a rumrunner's paradise—trucks laden with so much booze they crashed through the pier at Avila Beach, and agents doing their best in running gun battles down this way. It was also a time of shared poverty. Cars at one local dealership were selling for 99 cents each.

It's different here today, of course, with Arroyo Grande on its way to becoming a hot Central Coast property.

ATASCADERO–MORGAN HILL

A break in CA 1, from Cayucos to Carmel, will put you on inland US 101. So here's a little flavor for that route.

If, like millions of original and latter-day James Dean fans worldwide, you are fascinated by his life and death, you'll want to turn east from **Atascadero** on CA 41 (Southbound travelers would take CA 46 out of Paso Robles). Atascadero is the place where James Dean was officially pronounced dead at age twenty-four, and we may as well get that part over with.

The accident site is only about twenty-five miles east of Paso Robles, near the town of **Cholame** (*Sha-lom*). The population there is reportedly sixty-five, but only one or two are ever in evidence. Outside a small café that always looks as if it is ready to blow away is a brushed metal memorial placed under a shade tree by a Japanese fan. A few hundred yards farther east, at the confluence of CA 41 and CA 46 (formerly 466), is where the fatal accident occurred in the slanting sunlight of an autumn day in 1955.

A newer, wider highway is in place now, but if you look east, you'll see the old alignment and better understand how Dean's Porsche Spyder could have been hit by a driver who may have believed he had the right of way.

The accident has since been replayed by the press thousands of times, generally with the editorial conclusion that Dean was driving too fast and at fault. Now that account has finally been put to rest by a computer model that takes into account everything known about the collision.

This latest and most comprehensive finding is that Dean was not speeding, could not have been from the evidence, and is blameless in the matter of his own death.

After visiting Cholame, you can continue on into Paso Robles along CA 46, the route taken by the ambulance in which he died.

Paso Robles is one of those places that coast-dwelling Californians tend to dismiss. Driving through in the heat of summer, it is easy to succumb to an urge to keep on going until the drive is over. Too bad. Because this is a lovely town, with remarkable architecture, marvelous wineries nearby, and a host of reasons to linger awhile.

Not the least of which is Paso Robles Inn, a historic garden hotel with an open central courtyard, running stream, waterfall, and pool to grace the grounds. Historic inns are gluttons for maintenance. Fortunately, a dedicated few are committed to saving and expanding them, as are the present owners of Paso Robles Inn.

The present hotel was built in 1940 and is a perfect example of a Monterey-style inn—shady verandas, solid plank doors, a Hollywood diner-style coffee shop, plus a linen-table dining room and cozy lounge. At the time this inn opened, this was a pretty fair distance over two-lane 101 from L.A. Paso Robles Inn, then as now, made stopping an occasion, not just an overnight.

Paso Robles is also the center of free-range cattle ranching in California, and the inn has been the drink-

and-dine choice of ranchers for decades. But drovin' can be dry work, and after one dusty day, two of the local cowboys rode their horses right into the cocktail lounge at Paso Robles Inn, for an immediate beer.

Now, that story isn't so surprising to Route 66 fans who know that Erroll Flynn often rode *his* horse straight into the El Rancho bar in Gallup, New Mexico, when on location there. What will get your attention here, though, is that the cocktail lounge at Paso Robles Inn is on the second floor and the staircase to it is covered in Spanish tile! To mark the day, the bar is still called the "Cattlemen's Lounge."

Kids—okay, grown-up writers, too—enjoy skinnying in behind the waterfall, and strolling the shady grounds is a treat at sunset. Seasonal rates are moderate, from $60. (805-238-2660)

Just across the street is the town square, plus a host of period structures, including the Clock Tower Building, a charm in itself.

Farther to the north, **King City** and **Soledad** (yes, this is where the Soledad Brothers were held—you'll see the prison off to the right) appear, pass by, and recede in the rearview mirror. This is relentless farming country.

Morgan Hill is on the lower edge of Silicon Valley and is a workable blend of agriculture, venture capital, and high-tech. It is also home to a highly successful wildlife clinic: The Wildlife Education and Rehabilitation Center—the only center in the area permitted to care for native wildlife by California Fish and Game authorities.

NORTHERN CALIFORNIA

If the coastal area north of Santa Cruz is blocked or fog-bound, you'll again be on US 101 inland to San Francisco.

San Jose is a city, no doubt about that, and midwife to Silicon Valley. But for travelers, San Jose's main attraction is the Winchester Mystery House. This has been a classic tourist draw since first opening over seventy-five years ago. Now it's on the National Register, and keeps on getting better, as more of the house is opened for tours.

The story, if you don't know it, is this. Sarah Winchester, heir to the firearms fortune, was an eccentric (to be kind about it), and her particular obsession was with staying alive in the face of overpowering guilt—plus some bad advice from a spiritualist. Sarah believed herself hunted and haunted by the spirits of those her family's repeating firearms had killed. She also believed, however, that the spirits wouldn't punch her ticket so long as her mansion remained unfinished. After one hundred sixty rooms, ten thousand windows, blind closets, and secret passageways, Sarah died anyway. But you've got to give the match to her on points.

Winchester House, at 525 S. Winchester Boulevard, is open every day but Christmas.

Above San Francisco, the Mendocino coast has occasional landslides, but you can rejoin CA 1 via CA 12, 253, and 20, so this beautiful run is not completely lost. Storms, however, may keep you inland, so here is a taste of that part of the route.

Like most California towns, **Novato** has a strong Spanish heritage, but the area first became productive in the mid-1800s when two planters put in enough fruit trees to qualify as the World's Largest orchard.

Petaluma, the next stop north on the old Northwest Pacific Railroad, and on US 101, also claims World's Largest, except for Petaluma it's in eggs—thanks to an 1879 invention called the incubator. For some time, Petaluma thought about nothing but eggs, and before the Great Depression, there was more money on deposit in Petaluma banks, per capita, than any place on earth. Now eggs are being joined by software—as companies bail out of San Francisco and Silicon Valley. A digital omelet is an interesting thought.

Santa Rosa put all its eggs in the junior-college basket, when everyone else was ga-ga over universities. The town won. Santa Rosa College is not only an excellent school, by any measure, it has become world famous, and *the* model for similar programs.

This is also where Luther Burbank (who had nothing to do with the city of Burbank near L.A., which was named for a dentist) set up his world-famous lab in plant science. Santa Rosa's center for the arts is named for him.

Santa Rosa is near the center of Sonoma (wine country)—Buena Vista Winery, California's oldest, is here, dating from the 1850s—and the town has a number of good restaurants and lodgings. If you're a rail fan, don't miss the stone 1904 depot in Railroad Square, in the first block of Fourth Street.

Farther along, **Healdsburg** and **Cloverdale** go about their daily vinicultural and agricultural lives without much thought of tourism. And little need of it.

But **Hopland** is well into the work of re-creating itself as a destination point for visitors. Named for the vast fields of hops once grown here, now largely replaced by vineyards, Hopland is one of those places that breeds both surprise and mystery, as it fashions what it will become.

The Fetzer Vineyards are here and well worth a visit. Unpretentious, their business is winemaking, not tourism. Yet their tasting room and visitor center are exceptionally gracious. You'll also find a unique garden, reflecting Fetzer's commitment to organic farming—countless herbs, flowers, fruits, and vegetables grow here without pesticides, herbicides, or chemical fertilizers.

And Fetzer is the only winery in this country to handcraft their own aging barrels on site. All in all a remarkable place to spend a little time. Turn east at the school, follow CA 175 less than a mile, and as the road bends left, continue straight through the gates.

A study in contrasts, **Ukiah** is the largest city in Mendocino County, and yet maintains a semirural, small-town atmosphere. Quality of life is not an issue here. Like traditional values, it is a given. Tourism has had little effect on Ukiah and is not especially courted. For its residents, Ukiah makes the most of its border position between redwood country to the north and vineyards to the south, and is justifiably proud of its standing as one of the nicest towns in America.

ABOVE THE COAST

Another scenic-view yawner, right? Not these flights! Check 'em out for safe, truly memorable rides in superb vintage aircraft.

Against the vast beauty of the Pacific Coast, three places gain deeper emotional resonance when seen from the air: North San Diego, San Francisco, and the three capes near Tillamook Bay in Oregon. Plus the aircraft themselves are such beauties you'll be bustin' your buttons for days.

More than any other, the sound of radial engines above the West Coast marked the 1930s and '40s.

Radials were the predominant design then—with cylinders arranged in a circle for maximum cooling—and are still used when power means more than speed. A radial powered Lindbergh's Ryan, ad radial-engined aircraft from WWII still win their share at the Reno Air Races.

These are all good things to know when it comes to finding the best aerial viewpoints—and linking the thrill of flight over spectacular scenery, with the muse of history. Because more than anything radials are the voice of aviation's golden age.

The airplanes themselves are no less inviting: real glass

instead of the thin plexistuff that buzzes and blurs; richly padded seats; wood trim; and a king-sized instrument panel. Plus the panorama beneath a high, sheltering wing.

Men who love the burble of an American V-8, and women who know (or wish they knew) the throb of a big Harley V-twin are all drawn by the raw power of a radial engine. Even veteran jet pilots find themselves turning at the sound of a radial on take-off. Just can't not watch one.

Here's how you can wrap your tour, some history, and a grand adventure into one package—take a flight above the coast!

CARLSBAD

Barnstorming Adventures is the kind of operation that once flourished across America's heartland in the 1920s and '30s—men and women who love aviation and enjoy bringing smiles to the faces of those who ride with them.

And if you've ever felt a little uneasy at the thought of open-cockpit flying, this is the place to get past it. In daily operation since 1992—when the owners flew out of the snows of Pennsylvania and established a new base on the coast—they are expert at turning timid smiles into major grins.

Their radial-engined Travel Air 4000 seats two in the front cockpit, and a twenty-minute flight over Carlsbad's flower fields and the beaches is breathtaking.

If you're a closet throttle-jockey, you can go for some mock aerial combat, or dive on enemy tanks cleverly disguised as cows. Name your aerial fantasy and Barnstorming Adventures probably has it on the shelf. Rates are from $49 each, for two.

SAN FRANCISCO

Seaplane Tours gives you a three-for-one: a radial-engined De Havilland Beaver; water take-offs and landings from Pier 39 right next to Fisherman's Wharf; plus San Francisco on the half-shell.

Beginning with a spectacular fly-by of Alcatraz just a few hundred feet over the water, the 30-minute Golden

Gate Tour takes in just about everything—the city's sky-line, bay, bridges, and islands. Cost is under $90 for adults and under $70 for kids. Seaplane Tours operates seven days a week from 10:45 A.M. to late afternoon.

But if you're a fool for beautiful cities, romance, and a bit of the bubbly for a special occasion, make reservations for the Sunset Champagne Flight, which cruises the coast and returns just as San Francisco's lights appear in the gathering dusk—then go to the Top of the Mark to see it all again from the inside out. It's sheer magic

TILLAMOOK

So it's all socked in, with fog packed tight against the Oregon coast, and you came thousands of miles for a gray-out. It happens. But you can transform that experience into an enchanting aerial view of cloudfalls, with white mists pouring through gaps in the headlands to cascade into the sea below.

One of the few remaining sky gypsies, the owner/pilot of Tillamook Air Tours flies a beautifully restored 1942 Stinson Gull Wing, with a 300 hp radial, and a fully carpeted, sound-insulated cabin, with leather trim. It's like stepping into a Cadillac!

And when the throttle goes forward, the tail comes up—now. In little more than an instant you're in the air, headed for a magnificent tour of Three Capes Drive from 1,800 feet. Rates start at about $50 per adult. And by publication date, an open-cockpit Travel Air biplane will be fully restored and ready for passengers.

And as if the ride weren't enough, the Tillamook Naval Air Station Museum is just a few feet away. It's av-buff heaven.

BOOKS AND MEMORABILIA

Assembling California. John McPhee. New York: Farrar, Straus & Giroux, 1993. $12.95

If California, and the tectonically active Northwest, seem like a crazy quilt of faultlines, headlands, and strike-slip zones, John McPhee is a master at explaining what nearly defies understanding.

Classic Cars—Woodies: A National Treasure. Bill Yenne. Cobb, Calif.: First Glance Books, 1997.

This book is absolutely beautiful to look at, whether you are deeply into Woodies or not. And here's a little experiment you can do with it. After you've sampled a bit just to see what's there, do a quick thumb-through. Let only the black-and-white photographs register, seeing what Detroit in its own cocoon was really marketing back then. Then do another quick thumb, registering only the color photographs—seeing where and how the cars ended up . . .

A whole society changes right before your eyes: stylized subservience in shades of gray suddenly becomes a hymn to freedom in sparkling color. Awesome.

Coast Redwoods: A Self-Guided Tour. Janet Wood Duncan. Redwood Adventures, PO Box 1191, Boulder Creek, CA 95006. $4.95, plus $3 shipping and handling.

How did the redwoods manage to outlive the dinosaurs and survive—individually, and as close-knit families—for up to three thousand years? If you are unable to walk with Janet Wood Duncan in Santa Cruz, pick up the book and take your own tour through redwood country.

Sins of the City: The Real Los Angeles Noir. Jim Heimann. San Francisco: Chronicle Books, 1999. $18.95

Everything you suspected about Los Angeles—and knew better than to ask. In this tour of the (frequently dead) underbelly of L.A., author Jim Heimann pulls no punches and leaves no graves undisturbed. From Aimee Semple McPherson to Bugsy Siegel, this book serves it up. Pick up a copy and don't take no wooden nickels in change, yeah?

FOOD

Life on the road needn't mean waiting for a table at an over-priced beach bistro. One of the joys of traveling the coast is that a picnic or sundown barbecue is as close as the nearest supermarket—which usually has a well-stocked deli case. Grab some cool drinks and drive along until some beach or cove or forest glen calls out to you, and let nature serve up its best.

Roadwise travelers know that sitting in a car doesn't burn much in the way of calories. Lunch can easily be sacrificed, so many of the restaurants listed here are at their best for breakfast and dinner.

Astoria—**Shark Rock Cafe,** at Marine Dr. and 11th St. One of Astoria's best, with a terrific burrito that's a meal and then some.

Wet Dog Cafe, on the right on 11th St., is a hangout for locals. Right on the water. Children are welcome until 9 P.M. After that, folks tend to get into the music and the wonderful microbrews served here. Try the apricot ale, if they have it.

Cambria—Burton Drive is home to several excellent, if pricey, restaurants, including **Robin's,** with vegetarian-friendly fare and excellent service. **Creekside Gardens,** at 2114 Main St., is a very nice breakfast spot favored by locals, and **Moonstone Beach Bar & Grill,** at 6550 Moonstone Beach Dr., serves a fine brunch.

Capitola—Blessed by a number of excellent restaurants, try **Dharmas Natural Foods Restaurant,** at 4250 Capitola Rd. Dharmas has a strong local following and is well-known all along the coast. Or if *very* nice Italian is on your mind, the classic pesto and other dishes served up by **Bella Roma Cafe,** at 316 Capitola Ave., are somewhat pricey, but in every way, superb. Enthusiastic service as well.

Carlsbad—The Emerald Isle is rarely represented on PCH, but **Tom Giblin's Irish Pub** is a standout at 640-A Grand Ave. Great stews and Irish fare.

Coos Bay—**Benetti's Italian Restaurant** serves excellent fare, with a camp touch of gangsta from the servers. And if you can't decide, go for the Combo Plate, it's terrific. Small servings are available, if your car seat is beginning to complain. Moderate prices. Seating upstairs offers a view of the bay. Vegetarian-friendly. At 260 S. Broadway.

For breakfast and lunch, it's hard to beat **Pancake Mill Restaurant** at 2390 Tremont (US 101). Wonderful lattes and espressos, a pie shop that can drive travelers crazy, plus meat-free selections. Prices are low to moderate. Open every day, six A.M. to three P.M.

Del Mar—"Where the Turf Meets the Surf" sounds pretty steak-and-seafood, doesn't it? Not necessarily. **Garden Taste,** in 101A of the Del Mar Plaza, at 1550 Camino Del Mar, is a very nice vegetarian restaurant with organic, non-wheat dishes that will please all but the most dedicated meaties. Not just sprouts in a bowl here. Try the veggie burgers and the non-dairy pizza.

Eureka—Housed within the Carter Hotel, the **301 Restaurant** offers one of the finest five-course dining experiences anywhere on the coast. Fully half the menu is vegetarian-inspired and items may be ordered individually, if desired. Dinners from $14. And—brace yourself—the wine list comprises *2,000* vintages personally selected by the host. Exceptional, by any measure.

Forks—**Golden Gate Chinese Restaurant,** 80 West A St., is a good choice if you need a break from seafood. **The Smoke House,** a mile north of Forks on US 101, is great for steak and seafood. Or if you're a breakfast-anytime person, stop at the **Coffee Shop at Pay & Save ShopRite,** 241 Forks Ave. You'd never think to go *here,* right? But it's where local lumberjacks eat. Just head right into the market and hang a right into the restaurant. Captain's chairs at the counter and flapjacks the size of dinner plates. Real Babe-the-Blue-Ox stuff.

Gearheart—Whether you're in the mood for a sit-down meal or plan to dine *à la car,* the **Pacific Way Bakery**

and Cafe is a great little spot, with waist-buster baked goods.

Gold Beach—If you've noticed that veggie-friendly places are growing scarce, try **Soakers Coffee House,** 29844 Ellensburg Ave. (US 101), for organic coffees and baked goods. Lunches, too. Open seven days.

Laguna Beach—**Cafe Zinc,** at 350 Ocean, is the place to join the locals for breakfast, and if your lip is set for Mexican food, **Taco Loco,** at 640 S. CA 1 is better than most.

Long Beach, WA—For casual dining in an innlike atmosphere, with terrific food (all from scratch by a four-star chef), great prices, and relaxed-but-perfect service, it's the **42nd Street Cafe,** on Pacific in Seaview. Breakfast, lunch, and dinner, and your choice of full or half-portions—a blessing to carbound travelers.

Morro Bay—Most of the eateries are right on the waterfront. **Hoppe's Marina Square,** at 699 Embarcadero, along with **Harada's Japanese Restaurant,** at 630 Embarcadero, get consistently high marks. As always, though, check the menu for selection and prices.

Newport—**Cosmos Cafe & Gallery,** at 720 NW Olive St., just up from Elizabeth St., is tops for lunch and breakfast, with *awesome* lemon-zucchini muffins, super organic nachos, and a host of tasty selections.

A down-home place for breakfast or lunch is the **Courthouse Cafe,** on the west side of US 101 at Angle St., across from the Naterlin Community Center.

For a very special dinner, drive over to **April's at Nye Beach,** at 749 W. 3rd St., for a blend of Northwest/Mediterranean created by a former personal chef for Paul Anka. Moderate pricing and higher. Considered by locals to be tops.

North Bend—**Tai's Dynasty,** at 1903 Sherman Ave., offers a break from omnipresent seafood on the coast, and gets very good local reviews. And if you're feeling a little retro, the **Virgina Street Diner,** at 1430 Virginia Ave., is the place to go.

Novato—A very nice indoor/patio dining spot is the **California Grill,** at 1531-A S. Novato Blvd. Wood-fired rotisserie for chicken, ribs, and vegetables.

Oceano—The **Rock & Roll Diner,** at 1300 Railroad Ave., is a converted railroad car (rock and roll, get it?) that leaps right back into the 1950s with red-and-white sparkle vinyl and jukeboxes at the tables. Good breakfasts. Friendly service.

Oceanside—The restaurant scene has taken a great leap forward. **The Longboarder Cafe,** at 228 N. Coast Hwy., across from the California Surf Museum, serves vegetarian as well as standard fare. Grand omelets and oatcakes for the health-conscious child in you. Neat place.
  Love Mexican food, but hate the fat? Try **Johnny Mañana's,** at 308 Mission Ave., just up from the pier. Good burritos, fish tacos. Everything cooked lard-free.

Pacific Grove—**Tillie Gort's** is one of those places you'll wish you'd known about all your life. Both meatie and veggie preferences are well served at this friendly little storefront cafe. Moderate prices. 111 Central at Eardley.

Port Angeles—If you're health-conscious, the Northwest can be tough at times. Try **First Street Haven** for lunch. Unpretentious storefront, but excellent baked goods. On First St. at Laurel. And **Bella Italia** is excellent in every regard, with awards and travel-mentions to its credit. Just two blocks south of the ferry, at 117B First St.

Port Townsend—It's hard to go wrong in this town, so here are a few places you might otherwise overlook. For one of the top eateries in the Pacific Northwest, head for **Coho Restaurant** at 1044 Lawrence. Vegetarian—though non-veggies will be happy here—and environmentally supportive. Enjoy the regular art shows. This is a *wonderful* place.

Rest your tootsies and catch up on your e-mail at **Cafe Internet,** 2021 E. Sims Way, or have a quick lunch and a special treat at the **Plaza Soda Fountain,** in the back of Don's Pharmacy, 1151 Water St.

Reedsport—The **Windjammer Restaurant** has a great collection of model ships to munch by, at 1281 Highway Ave. And if you're screaming for ice cream, try **Don's Diner & Ice Cream Parlor** right on the highway.

San Diego—Along the Embarcadero, at 1360 Harbor Dr., it's hard to beat **Anthony's Fish Grotto** or the pricier **Star of the Sea Room.** These two go way back and are known for a wide range of excellent seafood dishes.

In Old Town's Bazaar Del Mundo, 2754 Calhoun St., **Lino's Italian Restaurant** is generally praised, or if you're ready for Mexican, **Casa de Peco** is good.

San Francisco—For period restaurants, it's hard to beat the moderately upscale **Shanghai 1930,** at 133 Stewart St.

For mystery fans there's **John's Grill,** with its Maltese Falcon Room and characters to match, plus a swell dame or two, located at 63 Ellis St. since 1908. The place was made famous by Dashiell Hammett, as a Sam Spade hangout, and it lives up to its reputation.

If Demon Burger still has you in his clutches, you can do no better than **Mel's,** at 3355 Geary Blvd. Although it is no longer a drive-in, the chrome-and-Formica ambiance works, and the shakes are great.

San Luis Obispo—If you enjoyed (or missed) F. McClintock's in Pismo Beach, you might want to sidle on over to **Izzy Ortega's Mexican Restaurant & Cantina** at 1850 Monterey, under the same ownership and a great place when you've got that lovin'-salsa feelin'.

San Simeon—The **Cavalier Restaurant** is a blessing along this coast. Excellent service and superb breakfasts, moderately priced.

Santa Cruz—A couple of places at the harbor may call to you. For end-of-the-day drinks, heated outdoor decks, and a view of the sailboat races on Wednesdays, the local hangout (plus emigrants from Silicon Valley) is **The Crow's Nest,** at 2218 E. Cliff Dr. All-around great place. Be at home here.

A short walk away along the yacht slips, at 493B (upstairs) Lake Avenue, is **Rosa's Roticeria.** Excellent Mexican fare with world-class salsas, plus veggie choices. Friendly buffet-style. Plan to take half your burrito home. Nice prices.

At the Santa Cruz Wharf, **Stagnaro Bros.** is the place to go for fresh seafood—they're also fish wholesalers—and this classic restaurant has been pleasing locals since 1937.

Santa Monica—Just a few blocks up from the pier, Santa Monica is blessed with perhaps the best vegetarian restaurant on the West Coast. **Real Food Daily,** at 514 Santa Monica Blvd., offers superbly prepared organic foods for every lifestyle. Even meaties enjoy the selection. What's more, in a restaurant genre given to cracker-barrel seating, the place is stylishly turned out.

Santa Rosa—Faith, and would ya be lookin' for somethin' tasty now? Head for **The Rose Pub & Restaurant.** It's a knockout. Play-along spoons, Irish Language lessons—and all delivered with a wink and a bit of the brogue. Excellent menu, with everything Irish, plus vegetarian selections. Open at 11:00 A.M. Tuesday thru Thursday, later on Friday, Saturday. Closed Sunday and Monday. At 2074 Armory Dr., a block east of US 101 from the Steele Ln. exit and a block south.

LODGING

These are friendly and well-maintained inns, motels, and B&B places well worth a stay. Some have a history with PCH. Considering their locations, often in prime destination areas, most offer excellent value. Several you'd never find on your own.

A special note on B&Bs: From Santa Cruz north, you'll find increasing numbers of charming B&Bs. Maintenance costs on historic properties are high and their rates will often be above local motels. But by the time you figure in $20 per couple for breakfast on the road, the rates look far more attractive. And if you are even moderately social, you'll find the conversation most agreeable—with serendipity a regular guest.

Astoria—**Comfort Suites** at 3420 Leif Erickson Dr. on US 30. Few chains offer more than a corporate presence. This well-run motor inn is one that does. Exceptionally well-maintained, the place is a delight, from the sea-lion chorus out on the bay, and the clangity-clang trolley, to a perfectly hosted—and plentiful—continental breakfast. From $69, less with your AAA card. Hint: Bring the tray from under your ice bucket down to breakfast, load up, then head on back to your room without looking like you need three hands. (800-228-5150)

Up on the hill at the eastern edge of town (still on US 30), it's the **Crest Motel** in a beautiful setting. Popular for years, reservations are a must. From $69. (800-421-3141)

Bandon—A very nice range of lodgings, many on the ocean, from the pleasant and newly expanded **Sunset Motel,** 1755 Beach Loop Dr., with rates beginning just above $50 (800-842-2407), to **Pacific House B&B,** 2165 Beach Loop Dr. (541-347-9526), and the quite elegant **Inn at Face Rock,** at 3225 Beach Loop Dr. (541-347-9441)

Brookings—**Beachfront Inn,** right on US 101 with beach access, is quite nice. Comfortable rooms with fridges and microwaves. If it's a sports night on television, this is a good place to be. (541-469-7779)

Cambria—There is a row of excellent lodgings along Moonstone Beach Dr., plus the delightful **Victorian Cottage by the Sea,** at 270 Chatham. Built in 1906, this was once the lighthousekeeper's residence at Piedras Blancas Station. Sleeps up to six for $135 to $190 per night. Favorable weekly rates. Through McLean Realty. (805-927-6163)

Or try **A Little Bit of Heaven,** B&B 2280 Trenton Dr. with its own meditation garden, nestled in the pines at $95. (805-927-1958)

Cannon Beach—Blessed with a wide selection of lodgings in a moderate price range, try the condo rentals at **Tolovana Inn,** 3400 Hemlock (503-436-2211), or choose the very nice **Cannon Beach Ecola Creek Lodge,** north exit to Ecola SP, 208 5th St. Both in the $70 to $120 range. (503-436-2776)

Coos Bay—**Coos Bay Manor,** at 955 S. Fifth St., offers fine lodging for $80 to $100. A Colonial revival-style home built in 1912, now on the National Register. Shaded by fine old elms, this B&B has blessedly quiet guest rooms, thanks to deep-pile carpeting. And baths are graced by old-fashioned shower heads the size of hubcaps. All is warmly and perceptively hosted. Turn west at Johnson St. to reach Coos Bay Manor on Fifth St. (541-269-1224)

Or turn east at Johnson, toward the bay, for the **Edgewater Inn,** Coos Bay's only waterfront motel. Quiet, very nicely appointed rooms, some with kitchenettes, and an indoor pool and spa. Moderate seasonal rates of $65 and up. (541-267-0423)

Davenport—The **Davenport Bed & Breakfast Inn** is excellent, at 31 Davenport Ave. (not that you need an address) with very nice accommodations beginning at $78. This place is an institution around here, and can also be a last-minute save if Santa Cruz is booked up. (831-425-4818)

Eureka—You might expect lodgings of special quality here and you'd be right. The **Carter House Victorians** and **Hotel Carter** are a collection of four marvelously restored or re-created classics near the upper end of Old Town, at 301 L St. Superb attention to detail plus an open, friendly style of service raise these B&Bs to international class. And the host is a master at what he does. Rooms and suites from $145 to $500. Very special indeed. (707-445-1390)

Eureka Inn is well-managed and friendly, but in the classic style of West Coast inns like the Benbow Inn and Lake Quinault Lodge. Reflecting its surroundings, the Eureka Inn is warmly wood-paneled. At Christmastime the inn becomes a center of holiday spirit for the entire community, with the annual unveiling of a two-story Christmas tree. You'll find much of that spirit here year-round. Nicely appointed rooms, pool, and spa. With three restaurants and three lounges you can't go wrong at the table. There's even a shoeshine parlor. Rates from $115, at 7th and F Sts.

Forks—How about a place in the woods? Head for **Huckleberry Lodge.** B&B accommodations or three squares a day. From $100, depending on season and accommodations. Just before the Calewah River, turn onto Huckleberry Ln., which becomes Big Pine Way, and continue. (888-822-6008)

Gold Beach—**Gold Beach Resort,** on the beach at the south end of town, with large rooms, indoor pool, and spa, beginning at about $80. (541-247-7066)

Ireland's Rustic Lodges offers charming units, plus fireplace cottages in a woodsy setting, and is a fine value at this price. Very homey, with rates beginning at under $50. Reservations strongly advised. This is a popular place. (541-247-7718)

Half Moon Bay—In the most senior of all the town's buildings, at 324 Main St., is the **Zabella House,** a B&B, with very nice rooms for around $75. (650-726-9123)

And for a place of startling design, warmth, and beauty, take the Medio Ave. exit, three miles north of CA

92, to 407 Mirada Rd. for **Cypress Inn on Miramar Beach.** Under the same ownership as Capitola's Inn at Depot Hill, this B&B is every bit as warm and impeccably managed, with the same attention to food service, plus spectacular views and a beach-house style that draws rave reviews from national and international publications—it's an extraordinary experience. Rates are $170 to $275. Reserve early for weekends. (650-726-6002)

Hopland—**Fetzer Bed & Breakfast** offers a range of lodgings from Carriage House and Cottage, with delightful rooms, many with spas, plus a few kitchens, plus the Haas House, home of prior owners, and a place of warmth and grace. Read in the library nook in front of a fire, take morning coffee in the screened-in porch upstairs. It's all very slow-paced and inviting. Rates are $120 to $175 with a nicely presented continental breakfast. (800-846-8637)

In town is the endlessly fascinating **Thatcher Inn,** in which sense impressions tumble over one another in an attempt to take it all in. There's a well-stocked bar and a grand dining room. But start in the library. It'll knock your socks off! You'll also be delighted with how baths have been added to rooms in an 1890 hotel that originally had none. Graciously hosted, a stay here would be a highlight on any tour. Out of a Victorian novel from $110. On US 101 in town. You can't miss it. (707-744-1890)

Ilwaco—In a fine old church, the **Inn at Ilwaco** is very pleasant, with fireplaces and lots of soul. Moderate seasonal rates: $59 to $189, at 120 Williams NE. (360-642-8686)

Pricier but absolutely wonderful is **China Beach Bed & Breakfast,** 222 Robert Gray Dr. If you've ever dreamed about a cottage right on the shore, this is probably the place you had in mind. Only three rooms: $189 to $229. (360-642-5660)

Lake Crescent—If you cannot stay at **Lake Crescent Lodge,** be sure to take a meal there or at least look around the lobby, which has a tavern look (and it was) plus an eclectic blend of rustic furnishings, Mission, and what-have-you. Figure a little over $100 per couple for most rooms. (360-928-3211)

LaPush—**LaPush Lodge** is as close to being part of this village, the land, and the sea as you'll find. Nothing fancy—they intend never to have television in the rooms—but very livable, with everything provided. Moderate rates. (800-487-1267)

Laguna Beach—Well into the 1960s, **Hotel Laguna,** at 425 S. CA 1, was *the* place for an attractive young woman, who happened to be having a dry spell, to find an interesting liaison. It may still be. Rates are seasonal: $80 to $165. And the place still displays that laid-back gentility it always has.

Long Beach, WA—**Boardwalk Cottages** offers ten charming units right next to the boardwalk at 800 Boulevard South. Fireplaces and some kitchens, $54 to $114 depending on season. (360-642-2305)

Farther up the peninsula, look for **Anthony's Home Court** at 1310 Pacific Hwy. N., where you'll relax with a sigh. Superb collection of antiques. Good value at seasonal rates of $40 and up. (360-642-2802)

Finally, the magnificent **Shelburne Country Inn,** B&B at 4515 Pacific Ave. in Seaview. There simply aren't enough awardable stars for such an impeccably run inn. It could be called perfect, but the owners are always improving it, so nearly perfect must do. $109 to $179 depending on season. (360-642-2442)

Montecito—**Coast Village Inn** is comfortable and affordable with midweek rates from $69. At 1188 Coast Village Rd. Exit Olive Mill Rd. northbound, and Coast Village Rd. southbound.

Monterey Peninsula—In Pacific Grove, two blocks from the beach at Lovers Point, is the charming **Centrella Inn,** at 612 Central Ave. at Forest. In an area famed for its Victorian-style inns, the Centrella goes the distance in service and style. Nicely appointed rooms and nostalgic cottages. Lush landscaping, private baths, wine-and-cheese hour, fine breakfast. Moderate rates for the area: $119 to $239. (831-372-3372)

Morro Bay—**La Serena Inn** at 990 Morro Ave. From the crisp and attentive desk service to heavily padded carpeting, this inn shows a flair for detail. Rooms are nicely appointed, with all the soap-dish amenities you'd expect, from less than $80. But have you seen origami-folded toilet paper? A masterful touch, though it's hard to know whether to use it or save it. Many rooms with ocean views, some with gas-log fireplaces. (800-248-1511) **Embarcadero Inn** is also very nice, on the Embarcadero, south of Marina St. From $95. (805-722-2700)

Myers Flat—**Myers Inn.** Built in the mid-1800s as a stage stop. If you're short on daylight and long on miles, this renovated B&B is only yards from the Avenue of the Giants, right off US 101, and offers a restful night, a continental breakfast, and a good start in the morning. (707-943-3259)

Newport—**Elizabeth Street Inn,** with a fireplace and full ocean view from every room, four stories above a pristine beach. Plus thoughtful amenities like separate fan/light switches in the bath, a spiffy laundry facility, and free continental breakfast. Comfortable and very well managed. Turn toward the ocean at Angle, bend into 2nd St. and continue to end at Elizabeth St. (541-265-9400)

North Bend—**Pony Village Motor Lodge,** at 1503 Virginia Ave., offers good value with comfortable rooms, close-in shopping. Seasonal rates from about $50.

Pismo Beach—**Best Western Shore Cliff Lodge** was the first motor inn built on the bluffs here, over thirty-five years ago. Seagrass, rock, and pine setting. Spectacular views. Very comfortable and well maintained, with water so soft it practically fluffs in the shower. At 2555 Price St., with seasonal rates from $79. (805-773-4671)

Reflecting this country's fascination with Thor Heyerdahl's great adventure, **Kon Tiki Inn** is a most comfortable oceanfront motor hotel with stunning views of the beach from every room, and easy access. Pool and spa, plus an entire building devoted to fitness. At 1621 Price St., with seasonal rates from $76. (805-773-4833)

Port Angeles—The **Angeles Inn Bed & Breakfast** offers a very pleasant stay in a contemporary residence. More private than most B&Bs. Rooms are spacious, virtually soundproof—and when was the last time you saw ceramic tile on the *ceiling* of a bathroom. Excellent breakfast. Moderate rates from $55 to $105, depending on season. Follow Race St. to 7th St., turn east to last drive and walk up to right. (360-417-0260)

    Uptown Motel is also pleasant, on a bluff overlooking the harbor, and moderately priced from under $60 to $139, depending on season. In the first block of 2nd St., just west of US 101. (360-457-9434)

Port Ludlow—If accommodations are unavailable in Port Townsend, spend the day there and stay overnight at the **Port Ludlow Resort and Conference Center.** Very pleasant, on the shore, and moderate seasonal rates from $75. (360-437-2222)

Port Orford—**Castaway Lodging-by-the-Sea,** located high on a cliff, offers all ocean-view suites and rooms, many with enclosed sundecks and kitchenettes. A great place to hide out if a storm blows through. At night, the lights of Gold Beach are visible. Excellent rates from about $45. (541-332-4502)

Port Townsend—This place could house half of Washington—and nearly does on weekends—with a wide range of excellent accommodations. But reservations are a must. You'll recognize **The Tides Motel** from *An Officer and a Gentleman,* but barely—it's been fully renovated. Right on the waterfront, with beach access. Seasonal rates from $68 to $135, at 1807 Water St. (360-385-0595) And yes, you can request the room where They Did It.

Salinas—**Laurel Inn** at 801 W. Laurel Dr. Comfortable, in a quiet neighborhood. Nicely appointed with gas-log fireplaces. Pleasant restaurant adjacent in an otherwise

food-challenged area. Minutes from Steinbeck Center by
an easy route. Rates from under $60. (831-449-2474)

San Francisco—Only sheer genius and the culture of San
Francisco could produce **Hotel del Sol.** Once a drab,
down-at-the-heels '50s motor inn, it is now alive with
color, whimsy, and a unique charm. Envision the new VW
Bug as a hotel, and this would be it! The staff and conve-
nience to a range of fine eateries make this a special place.
At 3100 Webster, a block south of Lombard. Moderate
rates beginning at $99. (877-433-5765)

Or, if you've been bed-and-breakfasted to the limit,
and crave a full-service hotel experience in an American
tradition, it's the **San Francisco Hilton and Towers.**
Park in front while registering. When you know your
floor, drive right up via the integrated parking structure.
Beautiful views, one of the best people-watching lobbies
around, and all the amenities expected with the name
"Hilton." Rates are $189 to $269. 333 O'Farrell St. at
Mason. (415-771-1400)

Santa Cruz—A very pleasant inn is the **Casa Blanca** at
101 Beach St. (enter up the hill on Main St.). Many rooms
with waterfront view, private balconies. Some kitchens.
Excellent evening fare and service in the dining room.
Awesome brunch. Take home some popovers. Responsi-
bly priced at $95 and up in season. (831-423-1570)

Looking for a small, very private inn? **Marvista** is a
spacious two-room B&B, just three miles south of the
Park Ave. exit for Capitola. And it's lovely. Magnificent
ocean views, comfortable fireplace rooms with king-size
beds, plus robe and slippers, and a hot tub to go with
them. Need to unwind and reconnect after a long drive?
This is a perfect place to do both. Friendly rates, too,
from $135 mid-week. 212 Martin Dr. (831-684-9311).
Exit CA 1 westbound on Rio del Mar Blvd. Continue just
over 1 mi. and turn right on Martin Dr.

INDEX